T0279902

HILL COUNTRY HINDSIGHTS

STORIES FROM A SIMPLER TIME

MICHAEL BARR

THE
History
PRESS

Published by The History Press
Charleston, SC
www.historypress.com

Fredericksburg Weekend. By R. Bolton Smith.

First published 2023

Manufactured in the United States

ISBN 9781467153522

Library of Congress Control Number: 2022947995

To Allen and Madeleine Oestreich.
They loved their home in Gillespie County and never strayed far from it.

Even though I'm descended from a pioneer Fredericksburg family (Heinrich Wilke and his kin), and even though I've written a lot of articles about Fredericksburg and the Hill Country (yes, pre-wineries), in reading this book, I definitely learned some things about the Hill Country that I didn't know. Barr has written a readable and interesting book, highly recommended.

—Mike Cox, *award-winning Texas author of forty nonfiction books and an elected member of the Texas Institute of Letters*

Like a lot of places, the beautiful Texas Hill Country "ain't what it used to be." Michael Barr has made it his business to chronicle those bygone days with stories about the people (including one former president), places, legends, recreations and libations that give the region its unique history and charms.

—Clay Coppedge, *author of* Hill Country Chronicles *and* Forgotten Tales of Texas

CONTENTS

Preface   9
Acknowledgements   13

1. The World Needs *Gemütlichkeit*   15
2. A Couch Potato's Guide to Climbing Enchanted Rock   18
3. The Willow City Loop   21
4. Celebrating the Vereins Kirche   24
5. Strolling Through the Gillespie County Fair   27
6. The Nimitz Hotel: Amazing Hospitality   30
7. O. Henry in Fredericksburg   33
8. Buck Taylor: King of the Cowboys   35
9. Mary Evans: Cowgirl Icon   37
10. Electricity Comes to Fredericksburg   40
11. Early Radio: Window to the World   43
12. Seventy Miles of Bad Road   46
13. Teamsters Were Fredericksburg's Lifeline   48
14. Sheriff Klaerner, Dan Hoerster's Hat and the Blind Horse   50
15. Saloons: Symbols of Frontier Culture   53
16. The White Elephant Saloon   55
17. Last Dance at Pat's Hall   58
18. Peter's Hall   61
19. Vaudeville: It's Not Just a Naughty French Word   64
20. Marking Time at the Palace Theatre   67

CONTENTS

21. Hoodwinked by Hollywood 70
22. Making Out at the 87 Drive-In 73
23. The Domino Parlor 76
24. The Tower 79
25. Sunny Side Hut 82
26. Standing in Line at Dietz Bakery 85
27. Iron Brew 88
28. The Fredericksburg Railroad 91
29. The Tunnel 94
30. July Fourth in Fredericksburg 97
31. Football Comes to Fredericksburg 100
32. Female Athletes Confound Experts 105
33. Alter Stoltz Solves an Image Problem at FHS 108
34. Nine Pin Bowling 112
35. Legends and Giants 115
36. J.L. Yarbrough: A Passion for Baseball 118
37. LBJ and the Politics of Barbecue 121
38. The Johnson Treatment 124
39. Stonewall Barbecue Honors LBJ 127
40. Deer Hunting with JFK and LBJ 130
41. Lyndon's Little Brother 132
42. Broccoli Sign Halts Bush Motorcade 134
43. A Valentine's Day Gift from Arthur Godfrey 137
44. Bob Hope Comes to Fredericksburg 139
45. Bob Hope Meets Hondo Crouch 142
46. Making House Calls with Dr. Keidel 145
47. Frank Van der Stucken: Tenderly Poetic 148
48. Felix Pehl and His Old-Time Band 151
49. Adolph Stieler: The Goat King 154
50. Fred Gipson's Treasures 157
51. Alfred Giles: Texas Architect 160
52. The Mud Daubers Return to Luckenbach 163
53. The Luckenbach World's Fair 166
54. A Night for the Ages at Cherry Spring Tavern 170

About the Author 175

PREFACE

When I first came to Fredericksburg as a young teacher in 1981, this part of the Texas Hill Country still had a European flavor. Although English was the dominant language, I frequently heard German on the street and in the teachers' lounge (where I quickly learned all the German cuss words). The local radio station broadcast church services in German. I met teachers my own age whose first language was German. They picked up English at school.

I loved my new home immediately, although I had some cultural adjustments to make. The Germans had a wonderful carefree attitude that was foreign to me, and I was confused by it. They enjoyed life. They had fun and didn't feel guilty about it. Even the preacher drank beer in public—a total shock to a guy like me, born and raised in the Bible Belt, where beer drinking was prolific but well hidden.

I discovered that the Texas Hill Country had more colorful characters—with more interesting stories—than just about any place I knew of. I think those characters emerged because this area was isolated for so much of its history. Travel in and out of Gillespie County was difficult before paved roads connected the Hill Country to the rest of Texas after World War II. Eccentricities, distinct patterns of expression and some peculiar behavior had a chance to develop in isolation, free of outside influences.

There were new and interesting things to do in the Hill Country, and I got right to it. I climbed Enchanted Rock, drove the Willow City Loop, hung out at Luckenbach, cut a rug at Cherry Spring Dancehall, drank the coldest beer in Texas at the store in Albert and two-stepped around the tree at Pat's Hall. I went to the Gillespie County Fair (the oldest county fair in Texas), the horse races, the Fourth of July Parade (hands down the best small town parade ever), the Stonewall Peach JAMboree, the Lights Spectacular in Johnson City and the Doss Fish Fry.

In the summer, when I wasn't working for Tony Knopp at the swimming pool, I went to weddings—if not the ceremony, at least the reception. Fredericksburg had the largest weddings I ever saw, and there was one almost every weekend.

For the receptions, the wedding parties rented either Turner Hall or the Pioneer Pavilion and brought in beer and barbecue by the truckload. As soon as Bill Smallwood's band or Boyd Harper's band tuned up, the party was on. Half the town showed up—invited or not.

By the time I moved to the Hill Country, Lyndon B. Johnson and Hondo Crouch had died, but you could still see an occasional celebrity if you kept your eyes open. I remember the thrill of seeing Lady Bird Johnson on the produce aisle at the old HEB store on Austin Street in Fredericksburg. A secret serviceman almost tackled me when I tried to run over to say hello.

I was the principal at Fredericksburg Intermediate School the day George and Barbara Bush came to town. The entire school lined up on Main Street to greet them. We were told that the most we would get was a wave as they drove by, but Mrs. Parker's class made a sign that stopped the former president in his tracks—something about broccoli.

Although outsiders like myself had been moving to the Hill Country for years, most of the people who lived in Gillespie County at the time were German and Hispanic and had been there for generations. There was a small but vital Black population whose families had been in the area for over a century.

As best as I remember, most of the businesses in Fredericksburg back then catered to locals. I actually knew many of the people I saw when I walked down Main Street.

But a big change was on the way. The Hill Country was about to be discovered by tourists, city folk looking for a good place to raise children and oil company executives from Houston looking for a place to retire.

The next thing you know, the price of real estate went through the roof. Oma's house in Fredericksburg became a bed-and-breakfast. Mercedes and Lexus automobiles outnumbered pickups. Highway 290 between Fredericksburg and Johnson City became "the Wine Road." Soon, the old buildings along Fredericksburg's historic Main Street commanded a rent that would make Elon Musk blink.

Don't get me wrong, I love the Texas Hill Country now, the way it is. What a great place to live. But my heart is in the old days, before this place became trendy.

Some of the stories that follow were told to me, some of them I read about and others I experienced for myself. Collectively, they are a road trip back in time to the days before B&Bs, STRs (short-term rentals), wine tours and sky-high property values made life complicated.

Michael Barr

Acknowledgements

T hanks to all the people who passed along stories to me by email, over the phone, at church, at the coffee shop, at bars and restaurants and at the grocery store. Those stories are the core of this book. Thanks also to R. Bolton Smith for allowing me to use his image *Fredericksburg Weekend* for the cover. It captures perfectly the anticipation of a trip through the Hill Country. *Gracias* to Ken Esten Cooke, the publisher and editor of the *Fredericksburg Standard*, who lowered his standards enough to print these stories the first time around. And a special *Danke* goes to Jimmy Reichenau. When I was staring down a deadline and needed something to write about, Jimmy always came through.

1

THE WORLD NEEDS *GEMÜTLICHKEIT*

*G*emütlichkeit is one of those uniquely German words that has no precise English equivalent. It is tricky to spell, and only a German can pronounce it properly. It has nothing to do with sneezing.

Google says Gemütlichkeit is a noun meaning "comfort, coziness or friendliness," but that's like saying Lyndon Johnson was a politician or Chester Nimitz a sailor.

Gemütlichkeit is a complex component of German social life. It goes to the heart of what it means to be German.

I have heard Gemütlichkeit defined as "that warm, friendly feeling that comes as a natural effect of a sociable evening spent in the company of family and good friends. It's about beer, food, music, laughter and conversation. It is a love of celebrations and the German way of life."

Another way of putting it is that Gemütlichkeit is a state of mind in which the *Gemüt*, the inner person, is satisfied. Whatever contributes to that state is Gemütlichkeit.

Long ago, in Germany, after hardworking farmers harvested their crops, they set aside a time in the fall to have fun. They raised tents and brought in oom-pah bands, beer and bratwurst. They danced, sang and partied hard. Gemütlichkeit came from those celebrations.

German immigrants brought the concept to Milwaukee, St. Louis and the Texas Hill Country. After working hard all week, German Americans spent Saturday nights and Sunday afternoons at beer gardens, ice houses and baseball games, soaking up a little Gemütlichkeit.

But there was another side to the story. A growing number of Americans believed the German fondness for beer, dancing and frivolity, especially when practiced on Sunday, was scandalous—even sinful.

The *New York Times*, that nineteenth-century voice of the eastern Protestant establishment, with its affection for Prohibition and blue laws, expressed the hope that German immigrants and their descendants would outgrow their Old World habits and learn to behave themselves like proper Americans. "In the old countries, where freedom is smothered, drinking may be necessary to drown the depressing influence of despotism; but here, where freedom woos the mind to culture, no such beastly compensation is called for, and we believe we have said sufficient to prove that our German fellow citizens are born for higher and nobler uses than for schnapps and bier."

New England Puritans snobbishly agreed. "It cannot be claimed," the *Times* article continued, "that its [St. Louis's] inhabitants are pious, in the sense of the word as understood in Boston."

Meanwhile, the Germans continued to enjoy themselves without guilt or reservations. An April 1883 article in *Lippincott's Magazine* explained:

> *Beer and wine the German looks on as gifts of God, to be enjoyed in moderation for lightening the cares of life and adding to its pleasures, and Sunday afternoon is devoted, by all who do not belong to the stricter Protestant sects, to recreation.*
>
> *[The Germans] burst from their homes on the Lord's Day, filling the streets with laughter and chatter, as they make their way to such umbrageous enclosures as beer gardens. Music, dancing, ball games and other amusements are indulged in with a zest which shows the intensity of pleasure realized from them by the participants. For them, such pleasures are "soul-feasts."*

The *Cincinnati Inquirer* went so far as to suggest that Gemütlichkeit, especially the consumption of German beer, helped civilize America.

> *Formerly, Americans drank scarcely anything else than whiskey, frequently very bad whiskey, and the consequence was quarreling, strife and fights. Now, Americans drink almost as much beer as the Germans do, and whereas Americans used to pour everything down their throats standing, they now sit down good naturedly and chat over a good glass of beer without flying into one another's hair.*

Gemütlichkeit means different things to different people. To me, it means life is short, so enjoy it. Lighten up. Have some fun. Savor the special moments and resolve to have more.

Our country is a little short on Gemütlichkeit these days. Both political parties could use some Gemütlichkeit. Maybe we should add a little to the drinking water at city council meetings. In fact, we all need a little Gemütlichkeit after the year we've had.

2

A Couch Potato's Guide to Climbing Enchanted Rock

When I first came to Fredericksburg many years ago, a friend told me he was going out to climb Enchanted Rock and invited me to go along. Well, climbing rocks is not my thing (climbing into a lawn chair on the riverbank with a six-pack and a fishing rod is more my speed), but since it was a Saturday and I had already ironed my underwear and rearranged my sock drawer, I tagged along.

I've made other trips to Enchanted Rock since then, and each time, I've seen something wonderful and learned something new.

I learned an important lesson that very first day: the cowboy boots were a bad idea.

Enchanted Rock has been the object of curiosity and wonder for centuries. Experts who know about such things say the granite dome first formed somewhere between 4.5 million and 540 million years ago, give or take a few millennia. It formed as molten magma from deep in the Earth and pushed its way upward, but for some reason, it stopped rising somewhere below the surface. After the magma cooled and hardened, centuries of exfoliation and erosion exposed the dome.

Enchanted Rock rises about five hundred feet above Sandy Creek, and its dome covers about one square mile. It is the second-largest granite mountain in the United States after Stone Mountain in Georgia.

Some history books say Captain Henry S. Brown discovered Enchanted Rock in 1829, but the truth is that Native Americans beat Captain Brown there by a few centuries.

Enchanted Rock. *Author's photograph.*

Enchanted Rock was a special place for Native Americans. The enormous granite dome supposedly made groaning sounds as it expanded in the heat of the day and contracted when the temperature cooled in the evening. Native Americans believed spirits lived there. To them, it was a holy place.

In the 1840s, Samuel Maverick, a signer of the Texas Declaration of Independence, hired surveyor James P. Hudson and two chainmen to survey eight and a half labors of land that included Enchanted Rock. The State of Texas issued Maverick a patent for the land in September 1851.

Maverick didn't give a hoot about spirits. He was after gold and silver but didn't find much. Those precious metals do exist in that part of the Hill Country but not in paying quantities.

For years, Enchanted Rock stood there as it always had, moaning and groaning and keeping watch over the rough country in northeast Gillespie County.

In the late nineteenth century, Reverend Dan Moore from Willow City held an annual church service on top of Enchanted Rock. Worshippers rode their horses or walked to the summit to hear the sermon based on Matthew 16:18: "Upon this rock, I will build my church, and the gates of hell shall not prevail against it."

The Moss family bought the property in 1886. Then sometime in the early twentieth century, the public discovered Enchanted Rock.

Beginning in 1927, Tate Moss opened Enchanted Rock to campers. The Moss family operated the place as a private park until the Texas Parks and Wildlife Department bought it 1978.

The park closed for eighteen months in the early 1980s while workers built campsites and marked trails, but the hikers and climbers kept coming. Authorities wrote three hundred citations for trespassing while the park was closed.

I remember a rumor going around that Enchanted Rock would become a second Mount Rushmore, with the faces of three prominent Texans carved into it. I'm glad that didn't happen, but if it had, I would have voted for Farrah Fawcett, Willie Nelson and Nolan Ryan.

Climbing Enchanted Rock is not all that difficult for a climber with healthy legs and the proper footwear. The climb starts out easy but gets a little harder as you go up. The domed shape of the mountain is deceiving. At several points along the climb, you think you are near the summit, only to get there and find you have a lot farther to go.

But once you reach the top, you are rewarded with a spectacular view of the Hill Country. At that moment, the climb is worth the effort, even for a guy like me, whose favorite climb is into a Laz-Z-Boy.

3

The Willow City Loop

The Willow City Loop is nothing like those massive, crowded, multilane, circular, concrete demolition derby arenas that encircle San Antonio or Houston. The Willow City Loop has no exit ramp, frontage road or flyover—not even an HOV lane, whatever that is.

No, the Willow City Loop is a narrow, mostly paved road that runs through some of the most spectacular landscape anywhere. If there is a prettier place in Texas, especially in April and May, when the bluebonnets are showing off, I don't know where it is. It's easy to get carried away by the scenery on the Willow City Loop, even as your allergies kick in.

A drive along the Willow City Loop is a slow rollercoaster ride through narrow valleys and over steep granite hills, cattle guards and low water crossings. Multicolored wildflowers hug the road, cover the pastures and crawl up the hillsides. Even the thistles, prickly pears and mesquites there are unusually perky and photogenic.

With good timing a traveler on the Willow City Loop will be rewarded with a bumper crop of bluebonnets, Indian paintbrushes, fire wheels, wine cups and white poppies. Climbing every hill is like turning a page in a picture book.

Throw in a herd of cattle lazily munching grass, some cautious white-tailed deer, a few tin barns and a couple of rusty tractors, and the Willow City Loop transforms into the most picturesque setting in the Hill Country. It is one of the most photographed and most painted places in all of Texas.

Willow City Loop. *Author's photograph.*

There are several ways to get to the Willow City Loop. From Fredericksburg, I take Highway 16 toward Llano, through the metropolis of Eckert, past Bell Mountain (you'll know it when you see it), and cross Legion Creek at the bottom of the hill. I then turn right at the first road past the Legion Creek Bridge, rumble across the cattle guard and you're there.

On that trip, you will notice that the countryside changes from grassy hills dotted with live oaks on the Fredericksburg side of Bell Mountain to a rockier and more rugged landscape with sharper edges as you approach the Llano County line. A lot of the soil along the loop is more like red gravel than dirt.

The road on the north side of Willow City through Coal Creek Canyon has been known locally as the Willow City Loop since at least 1950. It was a Hill Country secret for years until folks from Austin and San Antonio sneaked in and discovered it. Then journalists from the *Austin American-Statesman*, the *San Antonio Express-News* and the *San Antonio Light* let the cat out of the bag.

Although some area ranchers did private road work in the early twentieth century, that part of Gillespie County to the northeast of Willow City, including Coal Creek Canyon, had no public roads. Then in 1934, the Gillespie County Commissioners Court established a third-class road, forty feet wide, from the Holmes-Moss Ranch over to the Llano/Fredericksburg Road.

The process of paving the Willow City Loop began in the 1960s. Rancher A.F. Buie, the owner of the Serpentine Mine, donated material for the pavement. Commissioners completed the paving project in 1976.

Motorists are encouraged to enjoy the view along the Willow City Loop, but they should remember that this is a special place. Don't trash it. Stay on the main road and stay in your car. The right-of-way is mostly unfenced so deer and livestock can move freely. It's not an invitation to take an off-road excursion. Remember, the property is private on both sides of the road.

The Willow City Loop is nothing at all like its big city counterparts, although weekends in the spring can get a little crowded. Even then, the traffic along the loop is slow, peaceful and relaxing. The scenery is beautiful anytime of the year, but in the springtime, when Mother Nature is in a good mood, the Willow City Loop hosts the most breathtaking flower show on earth.

4

CELEBRATING THE
VEREINS KIRCHE

While Fredericksburg, Texas, is well known for its celebrations and festivals, the town may never top the wingding that was held on the day workers laid the cornerstone for the original Vereins Kirche.

After spending their first year getting settled on Baron's Creek, the Germans of Fredericksburg began constructing a public building in the spring of 1847. They called it Vereins Kirche (association church), an indication of its dual purpose as a social hall and a house of worship. Its design and central location were reminiscent of distinctive municipal buildings that often stood in public squares in Germany.

That spring was a busy time in Fredericksburg. John Meusebach had just negotiated the famous peace treaty with the Native Americans. For the formal signing, the Comanche chiefs appeared in Fredericksburg on March 9, 1847. Apparently, by coincidence, that was also the day workers laid the cornerstone for the Vereins Kirche.

A 1976 article in the *Fredericksburg Standard* described the scene from historical documents. The Comanche, "led by their chiefs, Ketemoczy and Santana, and some of their tribe, arrived in the village. They were arrayed in beaded buckskin attire and feathered headdresses. The Indians brought with them tanned hides, bear fat and deer skins filled with wild honey."

Not long after the Comanche arrived, the festivities surrounding the laying of the Vereins Kirche cornerstone began with a procession down Main Street. "First came the minister, the teacher and officers of the Adelsverein," the article continued, "followed by Vereins soldiers on

Vereins Kirche, Marketplatz, Fredericksburg. *Author's photograph.*

horseback and the small Vereins cannon drawn by four horses, with the citizens bringing up the end of the procession. After much oration and ceremony the cornerstone was laid in the opening left in the wall." Soldiers fired the cannon. Then the fun began.

The Comanche performed ceremonial dances in the street. Then everyone "drifted toward a dancing green that had been prepared under the tees."

"Near it was a platform for the newly organized orchestra and all around it were benches for the ladies. Just as the white settlers wondered in amazement at the Indian dances, so the Indians stood by in wonderment as the Germans swirled through their schottisches, waltzes and gallops."

When completed later that year, the original Vereins Kirche sat in the middle of Main Street between the old courthouse and Marketplatz. The town meetings and other activities within its walls soon became the heartbeat of community life. Children went to school there. Churches worshipped there. Couples walked for miles to be married there. The grand wedding processions marched up San Saba Street (now Main Street), followed by family and friends in the European custom.

The building had two doors. The men's door faced southeast, and the women's door faced northwest. In the fashion of the day, seating was segregated. Men sat on the right side of the aisle, and women sat on the left.

The walls of the original Vereins Kiche were made of wood, but after a few years, workers replaced the weatherboarding on the walls with limestone. At the same time, workers closed in the two doors and built a single door facing the courthouse.

The interior of the original structure was open to the belfry, but workers added a ceiling after bats got in and dive-bombed members of the congregation, disrupting evening worship. When a bolt of lightning knocked the weathercock off the top of the building in 1862, officials replaced it with a cross.

Then, over time, the different congregations in town built churches of their own. Town meetings moved elsewhere. By the mid-1890s, the old Vereins Kirche was an eyesore.

When Fredericksburg celebrated its fiftieth anniversary in 1896, workers removed the limestone blocks from the walls of the Vereins Kirche to build a pavilion. Within the year, the village tore down the skeleton of the old building so that Main Street, now the main thoroughfare between San Antonio and Mason could run straight through town.

The destruction of the Vereins Kirche left an ache in the heart of Fredericksburg. The community grieved until workers built a new one just in time for the Founders' Day party in 1935.

STROLLING THROUGH THE
GILLESPIE COUNTY FAIR

His craggy face was still grim but more relaxed than it used to be when its owner hung his Stetson on a peg at 1600 Pennsylvania Avenue. Hoping to mingle discreetly with the crowd at the Gillespie County Fairgrounds, Lyndon Johnson might have pulled it off, except for all those guys in dark suits and sunglasses who kept ordinary folk at a respectable distance.

Over the last 140 years, the Gillespie County Fair has had more than its share of exciting moments, none bigger than a visit from the thirty-sixth president of the United States, who strolled through the midway with his grandkids and his secret service detail.

The Gillespie County Fair dates to 1881. John Braeutigam hosted the first fairs at the site of old Fort Martin Scott. Braeutigam bought the property after the army moved out in 1866. The Breautigam family lived in one of the buildings and converted the officers' quarters into a dance hall called Braeutigam's Garten. It was the first dance hall in Gillespie County.

Fort Martin Scott was a natural place to hold a county fair. The old barracks became the exhibit hall. The parade ground across the creek was the racetrack. There were dances at Braeutigam's Garten.

Then in 1889, the Gillespie County Fair moved uptown to an area known as Central Park. The park occupied the area between Travis and Schubert Streets in front of the public school, where Turner Hall and the Coach Tony Knopp Swimming Pool are today.

The county held two fairs at Central Park. The attractions included athletic events, exhibits, a horse-powered merry-go-'round and horse races on a track several blocks away. Each day, just for fun, the ice factory froze a large bouquet of flowers in an ice block.

In 1892, a group of citizens formed the Gillespie County Fair Association. Later that year, the association bought forty acres of land across the creek (where HEB grocery store is today) from Peter Bonn. The asking price was $2,500.

The association constructed buildings to house exhibits and laid out a one-mile-long racetrack. Morris Ranch built the stables and tack rooms. Gillespie County held the first county fair at the new site in September 1892.

The Fredericksburg Giants often played baseball on fair weekend. The diamond was located on the infield of the racetrack. When a horse race started, the baseball game would pause, and the players would gather at the backstop to watch the finish. Once the race was over, play resumed.

While most fairs ran according to a schedule, the Gillespie County Fair occasionally went off script. On September 13, 1916, the fair association arranged for an airplane to fly in on fair day, but the plane crashed. Another year, so much rain fell on fair weekend the cooks buried the barbecue meat in the pits over which the meat was supposed to be roasted.

In the early twentieth century, Hermann Lehmann, a Comanche captive for nine years, was a star attraction at the Gillespie County Fair. He dressed in Native American clothing, danced and told stories about his time in captivity.

A baseball team watching horse races at the Gillespie County Fair, Fredericksburg. *Gillespie County Historical Society.*

In 1926, the fair association built a two-thousand-seat grandstand overlooking the racetrack. That same year, two teams played polo for the first time on the infield.

The fair hosted elephant races and hot air balloon rides. The fair association crowned the first fair queen in 1949.

When the railroad came to Fredericksburg in 1913, the fair association sold a two-hundred-foot-long strip of land at the back of the fairgrounds (along what is today Park Street) to the railroad for tracks and a depot. Then in 1975, after building the new fairgrounds on a 90-acre site along the Kerrville Highway, the fair association sold off the remaining 21.79 acres of the old Bonn property for $263,000.

Throughout its long history, the Gillespie County Fair has been a destination for race fans and a getaway for families. Even President Johnson couldn't resist the fast horses, Ferris wheel and cotton candy.

Then again, he always preferred the Hill Country to Camp David.

The Nimitz Hotel

Amazing Hospitality

The Nimitz Hotel in Fredericksburg is much more than the family business of Fleet Admiral Chester Nimitz. The old hotel was a local watering hole. It was a waystation and a gateway for the community. Visitors formed their first impressions of Fredericksburg from the warm reception they received at the Nimitz.

Charles H. Nimitz arrived with the early settlers in Fredericksburg. For a time, he was a cook at Fort Martin Scott. Some sources say he opened (or possibly managed) his first hotel at 218 West Main Street (the present-day site of the Schmidt-Dietz Building). A story in the *Fredericksburg Standard* (November 26, 1921) described that original dirt floor hotel as "a one-room structure built of adobe."

Although Fredericksburg sat squarely on the Texas frontier, a surprising number of travelers passed through in the early days. The town was a stopping point for stagecoaches on the road between San Antonio and El Paso. Soldiers on the way to West Texas forts stopped in Fredericksburg for one last civilized fling. The small hotel had a lot of business.

In 1855, Charles Nimitz built a bigger hotel at the corner of Main and Washington Streets. The new place had a large rock-fenced enclosure for horses. The *Fredericksburg Standard* noted the wall cost the fantastic sum of $150, not to mention the "free drinks of whiskey he had to furnish the men building it."

When finished, the new hotel had it all. There were three wells on the property. The building had wood floors made of cypress boards that were

Nimitz Hotel, 340 East Main Street, Fredericksburg. *Author's photograph.*

cut and hauled from the mill the Mormons had built and were operating on the Pedernales about 4 miles below the colony.

The Nimitz wasn't home, but it was darn close to it. Travelers willing to splurge could sleep in a bed by themselves. The outhouse was a short but polite distance away. The Nimitz was the only place between San Antonio and El Paso where a traveler could soak in a hot bath. At other frontier hotels, a guest could take a bath in clean water (unheated) for a dime or bathe at a discount if he was willing to "take a turn."

The *Fredericksburg Standard* reported that after the new Nimitz opened, "it became the place where the mail drivers of the U.S. Mail line from San Antonio to El Paso stayed. They found good quarters there and a fine place to keep their horses."

The hotel was a charming place with comfortable furnishings. On the walls were Hermann Lungkwitz drawings of Bear Mountain and Enchanted Rock. By all accounts, the hospitality there was amazing.

Quite a few famous people registered at the Nimitz. General Robert E. Lee and General Phil Sheridan stayed there. According to the *Fredericksburg Standard* "Dr. Ferdinand Roemer, whose studies for the new country were the first to be printed in Europe, made this hotel his home at various times."

William Sydney Porter, better known as the writer O. Henry, once slept at the Nimitz when he wasn't absorbing the local culture at the bar.

The Germans had a lukewarm relationship with O. Henry. They admired his talent but weren't always charmed with his treatment of their culture.

An article in the *Fredericksburg Standard* concluded "The beautiful story of 'The Chaparral Prince,' which uses as a setting the one time frequent mail robberies on the mail routes from here to San Antonio and which pretends to depict the life of the people of our country, was undoubtedly begun while the writer was at the hotel."

Charles Nimitz was a ship captain before he came to Texas, and by the late 1880s, he had socked away enough money to remodel his hotel to reflect his love for the sea. The wheelhouse of a Mississippi steamboat looming above the oak trees must have been a strange and mysterious sight for first-time visitors coming to Fredericksburg from Austin or San Antonio.

The hotel was a busy place in its prime. Prominent families from Houston and Galveston spent summers there. Locals had banquets and dances in the ballroom. The Lions Club, the Rotary Club and the Casino Club met there. The hotel was the center of social life in Fredericksburg for a century.

O. HENRY IN FREDERICKSBURG

The writer O. Henry was naturally curious. Wherever he went, he spent a lot of time soaking up the local flavor. His stories came from hotel lobbies, dance halls, saloons, park benches and lamp posts. Each story was a reflection of the world he was living in at the time.

Born William Sydney Porter in 1860, O. Henry was one of the world's great storytellers. At the age of nineteen, he moved to Texas from his home in North Carolina, spending time in San Antonio, Austin and Fredericksburg.

In San Antonio, he published a newspaper called the *Rolling Stone*. His readers enjoyed the poems, cartoons and funny stories, although the San Antonio Germans occasionally scolded him for what they perceived as unflattering images of their culture.

O. Henry came to Fredericksburg sometime in the 1880s to collect subscriptions for the *Rolling Stone*. Mrs. Dora Reagan, the granddaughter of Captain Charles Nimitz, recalled hearing her grandfather tell stories of O. Henry spending days at the Nimitz Hotel.

Just about everyone who likes to read has his or her favorite O. Henry story. My favorite, "A Chaparral Prince," came from that that road trip to Fredericksburg.

The story, in brief, is about Lena Hildesmuller, an eleven-year-old girl from Fredericksburg who was sent to work as a kitchen maid thirty miles away at the Quarrymen's Hotel. She worked hard—too hard for a little girl "no bigger than a frankfurter." Her only source of enjoyment, in fact, the only thing that kept her going, was spending her evenings with Grimm.

Then, one night, Mrs. Maloney, the lady who ran the hotel, took Grimm away. Mrs. Maloney, who was mean as a rattlesnake, claimed it was not good for servants to read stories about children lost in enchanted forests and gallant princes who rescued maidens from the witch's hut. Servants needed their rest, so no more Grimm.

Unable to carry on without Grimm, Lena wrote a letter, begging her mother to come and get her—otherwise, Lena planned to drown herself in the river. But the letter fell into the hands of an outlaw named Hondo Bill, who, along with and his gang, robbed the Fredericksburg mail wagon.

Hondo Bill was a tall, strong man with a soft voice, a rough unshaven face and a fondness for schnapps.

During the robbery, Fritz, the mail wagon driver, tried to shield Lena's letter, but Hondo Bill, his curiosity aroused, opened it. The letter was written in German, so Hondo Bill forced Fritz to translate it into English.

Before making his getaway, Hondo Bill tied Fritz to a tree. Fritz fell asleep, only to be awakened several hours later by Hondo Bill.

"Hit it out for home, Dutch," Hondo Bill commanded, untying the driver, shoving him into the wagon seat and placing the reins in his hands. "You've given us lots of trouble, and we're pleased to see the back of your neck."

When Fritz arrived in Fredericksburg, Frau Hildesmuller asked Fritz if he had news from her daughter Lena. Fritz told her about the letter.

Believing Lena may have drowned, Frau Hildesmuller began to cry. Then she heard a faint voice coming from the rear of Fritz's wagon. There was little Lena, half asleep, hidden among the mail sacks.

Frau Hildesmuller's sobs turned to tears of joy.

No one was more surprised to see Lena than Fritz. "How did you get in the wagon?" he asked. "The prince brought me," Lena replied.

I always knew he would. Last night, he came with his armed knights and captured the ogre's castle. They broke the dishes and kicked down the door. They pitched Mr. Maloney into a rain barrel and threw flour all over Mrs. Maloney. Then the prince came up, wrapped me in bedclothes and carried me away. He was tall and strong. His face was rough as a scrubbing brush. He had a soft, kind voice, and he smelled like schnapps. I fell asleep in his arms and woke up here.

"Rubbish," cried Fritz. "Fairy tales."

"The prince brought me," Lena said.

BUCK TAYLOR

King of the Cowboys

For most of the nineteenth century, the word *cowboy* was a derogatory term, attached to desperadoes and shiftless range bums who roamed the West, but a tall ranch hand from Fredericksburg helped transform the cowboy from an outlaw into a cherished American icon.

William Levi "Buck" Taylor was born in Fredericksburg, Texas, on October 15, 1857. His father died in the Civil War, and his mother died soon after. Various friends and relatives raised the three Taylor children: Mary, Buck and Baxter. Mary grew up in Willow City.

Buck learned to ride horses and work cattle at an early age. Like many in his profession, he was a drifter. The unattached romantic life was one of the advantages of his line of work. That freedom to come and go on a whim was one of the allowances made to cowhands by ranchers in exchange for short pay and few benefits.

In the 1880s, Buck drifted north to Nebraska. While working on Major Frank North's cattle ranch on the Dismal River near North Platte, Buck met North's flamboyant partner, William Frederick "Buffalo Bill" Cody.

Cody, along with everyone else, was impressed with the tall Texan. At a time when the average height of a man was well under six feet, Buck Taylor stood six feet, four inches tall. He was handsome and athletic, with wavy, shoulder-length hair. He could rope and throw a wild steer and ride the rankest mustang with astonishing ease.

When Buffalo Bill began his *Wild West Show* in 1883, Buck Taylor was the first ranch hand Cody hired.

Buck Taylor toured the world with *Buffalo Bill's Wild West Show*. He rode broncs and performed amazing tricks on horseback. Cody billed him as the "King of the Cowboys."

Buck became a major star, along with Annie Oakley and Sitting Bull. Fans mobbed Buck when he walked down the street in New York, London and Paris.

As Buck's fame grew, Cody upgraded Buck's image. Buck began appearing in public wearing fancy embroidered vests, spotted chaps and a pearl-handled six-shooter.

Cody, of course, wasn't interested in truth. He wanted to sell tickets, and he created alternative facts to suit his purpose. The transformation of the cowboy from fact to myth had begun.

Newspaper stories planted by Cody described Buck as "the brave orphan boy from Texas," pure at heart and always fighting for good. He was strong but shy. He was tough as nails yet "amiable as a child" and always kind to women.

Then, in 1890, western writer Prentiss Ingraham was searching for the subject of his next story. Ingraham wrote dime novels, a wildly popular genre of hastily written fiction issued in cheap paperback form for mass market consumption. Buck Taylor, the handsome western cavalier, was the perfect choice.

Ingraham produced a series of dime novels featuring "Buck Taylor, King of the Cowboys." Titles included "The Prince of the Lasso," "The Saddle King" and "Red Riders of the Rio Grande." Ingraham's fictional cowboy was no longer a villain but a medieval hero, slaying bad guys and rescuing damsels in distress.

The image caught on and began to spread. Just as the Buck Taylor dime novels hit the street, romanticized images of the cowboy, painted by Frederick Remington and Charlie Russell, grabbed the attention of the public.

In 1902, Owen Wister published *The Virginian*, a novel that established the classic western format used in books and western movies throughout the twentieth century. Zane Grey's western novels, with the cowboy as the hero, sold 40 million copies and inspired 112 movies.

Just as the era of the real cowboy came to an end, the era of the romantic cowboy began. By the turn of the twentieth century, the cowboy had been transformed from a no-good outlaw into a knight on horseback, the purest symbol of courage, honor, chivalry and individualism.

By 1950, the transformation was complete. The cowboy had become the symbol of everything good about America and the central figure in the American myth.

It all began with Buck Taylor, the original cowboy hero.

Mary Evans

Cowgirl Icon

The cowboy is arguably the most familiar character in American popular culture, but the cowgirl is a horse of a different color. Most of us have a glossy mental image of a cowgirl in rhinestones and a fringed jacket, but that image is a myth crafted by television and the movies. Women who grew up working cattle for a living had a little less sparkle and a little more grit.

Mary Taylor was a real Texas cowgirl. She was a lady who was the equal of just about any man when it came to riding, roping and running a ranch.

She was born on November 11, 1853, on a farm near Centerville in Leon County, Texas. Her parents died when Mary was young. An aunt from Willow City took Mary in and raised her.

Mary had two younger brothers who grew up to be famous cowboys. Baxter Taylor's specialty was bustin' broncs. Buck Taylor became a star in *Buffalo Bill's Wild West Show*. He was the subject of dime novels. People all over North America and Europe knew him as the King of the Cowboys.

Sister Mary could do just about anything around the ranch her brothers could do. By the time she was thirteen years old, she could rope steers and ride broncs. She was a crack shot with a rifle.

Like her brothers, she liked to show off. A newspaper story told of the time she rode a paint horse to the top of Enchanted Rock.

On October 12, 1870, Mary Taylor, aged sixteen, married Thomas Andrew Evans, a thirty-six-year-old Confederate veteran and stock raiser. Mary and Tom lived and worked on the William Shelton Ranch on Crabapple Creek, five miles from Willow City. A few years later, they started their own cattle ranch near Nebo Mountain, three miles north of Eckert in northeast Gillespie County.

The 1870s were the days of the open range and the Hoo Doo War. Outlaws and rustlers roamed the Hill Country. It was a tough time to be in the cattle business.

Mary worked day and night to keep the ranch afloat. She cooked, kept the house and worked cattle. She milked up to thirty-five cows a day. She gave birth to nine children. I wonder where she found the time. When her husband died in 1900, Mary added ranch manager to her resumé.

Mary's skills on horseback were known all over the Hill Country. The *Fredericksburg Standard* described her as "an expert horsewoman" who "knew the range as well or better than any of the ranchmen of her section. She was a typical western lady, and the stranger within her gates was always given a cordial welcome and true western hospitality."

Mary Evans's headstone, Willow City Cemetery. *Author's photograph.*

Early in the morning on September 10, 1918, Mary started for Fredericksburg in a hack pulled by a team of horses. She got to town around eleven o'clock, bought seed wheat and a load of groceries and was on her way back to the ranch by noon. Her children expected her return by midafternoon, and when she was late, her son Louis went looking for her.

Just after sundown, Louis found his mother lying dead in a pasture about two miles from the ranch. Groceries were scattered across the pasture. The horses grazed quietly a short distance away, still hitched to the hack. There was no evidence of a runaway or foul play.

Justice A.W. Petmecky of Fredericksburg held an inquest at the scene. He ruled her death an accident. Mary Evans had asthma, and the best guess was that she had an asthma attack and fell from the vehicle. One of the rear wheels rolled over her.

Joe Schaetter & Son of Fredericksburg prepared her body for burial at Willow City Cemetery.

"The death of Mrs. Evans," a writer for the *Fredericksburg Standard* lamented, "marks the passing of one of the most picturesque characters in this section of Texas."

Cowboy heroes in popular culture are too numerous to count, but cowgirl icons, like Mary Taylor Evans of Willow City, are few and far between.

ELECTRICITY COMES TO FREDERICKSBURG

The electricity that breathes life into our modern world comes to us through a complex system of generating stations and power lines. That system, the modern electric grid, doesn't have a single point of origin. It began with small grids scattered all over the country that combined and grew like crabgrass into an interconnected network.

Fredericksburg's electric grid began in 1896, when Alfred van der Stucken, Franz Stein, Adolph Gold, Charles Nimitz and Charles Schuwirt formed the Fredericksburg Electric Light Company. The company purchased a fifty-kilowatt generator and housed it in Rudolph Eckert's cotton gin on the banks of Baron's Creek (near Natural Grocers on East Main).

Cotton gins often housed electric plants in those days. The steam engine that powered the gin also powered the electric generator.

The light company's distribution system was a string of electric lines from Eckert's Gin along Main Street for two miles, with taps one block long in each direction on cross streets. The poles were long cedar posts with pine cross arms.

The electric company was up and running in time for Fredericksburg's fiftieth anniversary celebration in 1896, but on a test run, the load was too much for the small steam engine. The lights flickered on and then went out. The company asked customers to not burn their lights on the evening of the celebration so that enough electric power would be available for the program at Marketplatz.

On December 15, 1896, the Fredericksburg Electric Light Company bought a lot on the southeast corner of the public school grounds (near the present-day middle school). The company then bought a ninety-five-horsepower steam engine and moved the generator from Eckert's cotton gin to the new location. With the new equipment, customers had fairly reliable electricity every evening from sundown until midnight.

In 1915, the company installed a sixty-two-and-a-half-kilowatt generator and new steam boiler. The additional power allowed customers to have electricity from 5:00 a.m. to daylight, sundown to midnight and all day on Wednesdays so housewives could do their ironing.

The grid continued to improve, and by 1919, the electric company, now owned by Ernst Wilke, Willie Borchers and Felix Wilke, made electricity available to customers from 5:00 a.m. to midnight.

Then, on February 25, 1921, a fire destroyed the power plant. For the next thirty days, Fredericksburg had no electricity, except for a few homes and businesses that were connected to small private power plants operated by Klaerner's Opera House and Peter's Hall.

In March 1921, a group of twenty stockholders put up $2,000 each to form Citizens Light and Power Company. The company acquired the necessary

Citizens Light and Power Company, 302 East Ufer Street, Fredericksburg. *Author's photograph.*

equipment to restore electricity in time for the seventy-fifth anniversary of Fredericksburg in the spring of 1921. Again, the company asked customers to not burn their lights that evening so the company would have enough juice to power the celebration.

Later that year, the company built a new plant on East Ufer Street, across from Stein Lumber Company. The new generators went online on February 1, 1922. Since that time, the city has had fairly reliable twenty-four-hour-a-day electric service, although it was common in the early days to shut down the system for a couple of hours on Sunday mornings for maintenance.

In 1923, the company purchased two new 180-horsepower Busch and Sulzer diesel engines. Each engine weighed fifty thousand pounds and cost about $20,000. One engine ran the generator. The other engine was a backup.

In an amazing display of reliability, customers had twenty-four-hour-a-day electric service without a single interruption from November 1923 until October 1924, when operators forgot to fill the fuel tanks.

Then in the1920s and 1930s, the small electric companies all over the country began to consolidate. On February 1, 1926, Citizens Light and Power Company stockholders sold their stocks to the West Texas Utilities Company for $190,000, a nice return on a $40,000 investment.

Soon, transmission lines began bringing electricity to Fredericksburg from distant power plants. In 1943, the Texas Company, later Texaco, bought the diesel engines housed on East Ufer Street for $9,000.

By the 1960s, affordable, reliable electricity was the norm.

Today, flipping a switch is like turning on a faucet. We do it without thinking.

11

EARLY RADIO

Window to the World

On May 5, 1933, someone inside the Leo J. Blanchard Sporting Goods Store in Fredericksburg (located in the old Dietz Bakery building) threw a switch. I've probably watched too many Frankenstein movies, but I like to think that the lights dimmed and sparks flew. There was a faint but noticeable humming sound followed by the smell of something burning. Seconds later, Fredericksburg's first radio station was on the air.

The 1930s were the Depression years, but they were also radio's golden age. Stations were popping up all over the country. At the same time, radio sets were becoming smaller and more affordable.

Radio was the gin and tonic that helped many Americans forget their economic troubles. Radio brought music and laughter and lessened the feeling of isolation in rural communities like Fredericksburg. People who had never been out of Gillespie County could, with a radio and a little imagination, have box seats at Wrigley Field or be front and center at Radio City Music Hall.

Americans loved radio. Every town, large and small, wanted its own radio station.

Fredericksburg's first station, call letters WTTH, reached Kerrville, Harper, Mason, Llano and Johnson City. The station operated during the daylight hours. A lot of its programming was live music and local news.

But the early radio business was precarious, and by 1937, radio station WTTH was gone. John Segner opened a watch and jewelry repair shop in the vacant space.

For nine years, Fredericksburg had no local radio station. Then in 1946, the Federal Communications Commission approved the plan of the Gillespie Broadcasting Company to build a 250-watt station in Fredericksburg. Stockholders in the company included local businessman Walter McKay, attorney Arthur Stehling and Jerry Fisher, an experienced radio man who doubled as station manager.

The studio, control room and office complex of the new station were located in four former Plaza Hotel rooms on the second floor of the Security State Bank building at the corner of Main and Crockett Streets. The 150-foot-tall transmitting tower was located two miles to the northwest.

Work on the new station began in September 1946. At the studio and office complex, technicians installed soundproofing, a Gates console with two turntables and an Associated Press teletype machine. The teletype operated twenty-four hours a day, transmitting news from all over the world at a rate of sixty words a minute.

Workers completed all the remodeling and construction in November. After testing the system and getting final approval from the FCC, station KNAF, "The Voice of the Texas Hills," 1340 on your radio dial, began broadcasting on November 26, 1946, two days before Thanksgiving.

The broadcast day at KNAF began at 6:30 a.m. and ended at 10:00 p.m., Monday through Saturday, with slightly shorter hours on Sunday. Programming featured a fascinating lineup of music, drama, sports, comedy and news.

Music programs, in fifteen-minute segments, included Kate Smith, Bing Crosby, the Andrews Sisters, Two-Ton Baker the Music Maker, the Texas Drifter (real name Goebel Reeves) and Polka Time. Thirty-minute dramas featured *Sherlock Holmes*, *Tom Mix*, *True Detective* and *Superman*. One of the most popular local shows was the *Trading Post*, during which listeners could "buy, sell or trade anything."

On January 23, 1959, KNAF increased its power from 250 watts to 1,000 watts and transferred its frequency from 1340 to the now familiar 910. At the same time, an addition to the tower took it to a height of 245 feet, allowing signals to reach listeners in San Antonio, Austin and New Braunfels.

KNAF became a part of daily life in the Hill Country. DJs Jimmy Dunne, Curtis Short and "The Girlfriend" Alene Fritz were like family.

In 1966 George Riba, a junior at Fredericksburg High School, talked Norbert and Alene Fritz into giving him a job as a DJ. After graduation, George went to Dallas and spent thirty-seven and a half years as a sports reporter at WFAA-TV.

KNAF DJs Alene
Fritz at the mic.
*Gillespie County
Historical Society.*

There were worries that television would kill radio, but that never happened. There is something about radio that is still powerful and relevant today.

Radio is intimate and personal. With radio, you can be all alone and still have a friend in the room. Close your eyes, and it's easy to imagine you are at Carnegie Hall, Broadway, Yankee Stadium, the Ryman Auditorium or Woodstock.

The magic of radio comes in through the ears. The listener supplies the images with his own imagination.

12

SEVENTY MILES OF BAD ROAD

A trip by car from Fredericksburg to San Antonio in the early twentieth century was not undertaken on a whim. In fact, *trip* was too simple a word to describe the experience. It was a journey filled with surprises around every turn, attempted by only eccentric adventurers who enjoyed the thrill of living dangerously.

Before World War I, most Hill Country roads were horrible. There were few bridges. Cars were unreliable and underpowered. One old-timer compared a Fredericksburg to San Antonio excursion to "roller skating over the Alps."

In December 1916, Robert Penniger, the editor of the *Fredericksburg Standard* and *Wochenblatt*, drove from Fredericksburg to San Antonio in a Maxwell touring car. Penniger described the ordeal for his readers, many of whom had never been beyond their homes in the Pedernales Valley.

In those days, a smart motorist hoped for the best but prepared for the worst. For a jaunt over any distance, drivers packed lunch, emergency food and water, matches, blankets in the wintertime, an extra can of gasoline (remember, there were no gas stations) and all the equipment needed to fix a flat tire.

On that cool December morning, the Maxwell, anticipating the coming adventure, fired miraculously on the first crank, and editor Penniger rolled out onto Main Street. He splashed across Baron's Creek east of town, motored past the ruins of old Fort Martin Scott and then swung south, following what would today be the Old San Antonio Road.

To call it a road was a stretch. It was two parallel wagon ruts.

After crossing the Pedernales, the editor made good time through the bottom land, up the hill to Cain City and on to Grapetown, but upon reaching Bankersmith, his progress slowed dramatically. Recent rains had washed out large chunks of the road, leaving "big muds holes, rivulets and hog wallows." The car bounced along at a snail's pace, "a-bumping and a-jolting like a bucking bronco."

Terrible road conditions continued up the High Hill to the Alamo Springs Railroad Station. At the summit, Penniger saw the "polished piece of the Bear Mountain erected by the Nagel Bros. as a memento to drive carefully, else you might land in the graveyard." He hoped it wasn't a sign of things to come.

"From the summit," Penniger continued, "you can look way down into Kendall County, almost to the county seat, from where help has to come pretty soon or you never will see these sights again; the slopes of the mountain getting so bad that you will have to use a burro to get over this road."

There is a harsh beauty to the land on the back side of High Hill, but the road there was the roughest part of the journey. It was barely wide enough for a single vehicle as it zigged and zagged along the side of a steep, rocky incline. The Maxwell was "bucking up and down hills, along a precipice that spells broken limbs if your gas wagon don't keep to the righteous and narrow path allotted for trespassing. What you can do if you meet somebody coming toward you, I don't know; luckily I've never had to find out."

Then, after fording "Breite Creek, Schindel Creek, Block Creek and several other young ones that have no names yet, you reach the beautiful Guadalupe River." The crossing was one hundred feet of rushing, swirling water marked by some dead trees, "and if you don't hit it just right, you will get stuck and require a foot bath, some replacement of good language and a mule team to reach August Offer's palace and refreshment emporium at Waring."

After crossing the Guadalupe in fine shape, the editor reached Boerne at noon, and there, he stopped on the side of the road for lunch. He found the road in good repair, recently graveled, allowing him to "romp on the gas" and make good time. He reached his destination at three o'clock in the afternoon. For the seventy mile trip, he averaged ten miles per hour.

"Bad roads," the editor concluded, "are propagators of bad language and are degeneratory to good morals, automobiles, wagons, glassware, carriages, millinery and derby hats."

13

Teamsters Were Fredericksburg's Lifeline

A teamster sometimes found it necessary to use indelicate language to coax a team of tired mules pulling a heavy freight wagon up a steep hill. Flattery and sweet talk wouldn't get the job done. Mules had to know the teamster meant business. It has been said more than once that a teamster's most useful skill was his ability to cuss.

Before the railroad came to Fredericksburg in 1913, teamsters were the community's lifeline. Every consumer item not produced locally had to be freighted in over rough country from a considerable distance.

The earliest teamsters used oxen to haul freight to Fredericksburg and Fort Martin Scott, but by the 1880s, they had switched to mules and horses. Oxen were strong, reliable and could pull a lot of weight, but they never got in much of a hurry.

A trip by ox wagon from Fort Martin Scott to Fort Mason, a distance of forty-five miles, took most of a week. A trip from Fort Martin Scott to Fort McKavitt, a distance of ninety-five miles, could take two weeks, depending on weather conditions.

By contrast, a freight wagon pulled by horses or mules could, with a little luck, make the trip from Fredericksburg to San Antonio, a distance of seventy-five miles, in about four days, as long as the teamster didn't come down with laryngitis.

When hauling with oxen, teamsters walked beside the animals, shouting encouragement like Tarzan with his loincloth on fire. When hauling with horses or mules, teamsters usually rode the wheel animal.

While government teamsters hauled freight to Fort Martin Scott, over on Town Creek, the Fredericksburg Germans organized their own freight lines.

At first, teamsters hauled freight to the Hill Country from Indianola. Later, they hauled cargo to Fredericksburg from San Antonio and Austin. They traveled as far west as Big Spring and as far east as Waco.

Teamsters hauled lumber, wire, nails, feed, flour, cornmeal, sugar and bacon. Sometimes, the wagon bulged with kegs of beer that were hauled from one of the breweries in San Antonio.

A teamster's life wasn't for sissies. His bed was a blanket on the ground with a sack of corn for a pillow. He ate a lot of cornbread and bacon, along with whatever game he could kill and roast over a campfire. What his diet lacked in flavor, it made up for in cholesterol.

Weather, particularly in the winter, could be brutal for teamsters. Julia Estill wrote that William Kammlah suffered so much from the cold, "he lost all his toes on both feet. Another man was so cold, his companions thought he was dead. He revived after vigorous rubbing and never realized he had been frozen stiff."

And yet, despite the hardships, some men couldn't resist the lure of the wagon trail. Henry Hotopp made an estimated one thousand round trips between Fredericksburg and San Antonio.

Not only did teamsters need an iron stomach and a salty vocabulary, they had to be absolutely trustworthy. In addition to freight, they carried letters, personal items and important documents. "Fellow townspeople entrusted them with important messages to friends along the way," Julia Estill wrote, "and money to pay bills to wholesale houses in the city."

Teamsters sometimes hauled canvas bags full of silver dollars guarded by watch dogs. They hauled money hidden in nail kegs, bound for San Antonio banks.

Then in 1913, the railroad came to Fredericksburg. Trains, along with trucks and paved roads, put teamsters out of business.

The teamsters were a distant memory when, on May 8, 1935, a group of the old guys watched a parade on Fredericksburg's Main Street. The sight of old teamster Willie Knopp Jr. driving by in a freight wagon inspired them to organize an Old Teamsters' Reunion.

Klaerner's Park on the Harper Highway hosted the first reunion on July 20, 1935. Representatives of sixty old teamster families showed up. The group met annually for the next forty years.

Today, trucks are Fredericksburg's lifeline, and while trucks are easier to handle than horses or mules, I know a couple of truck drivers whose language could make a teamster blush.

It's good to know some of the old ways still apply.

14

Sheriff Klaerner,
Dan Hoerster's Hat and
the Blind Horse

Gillespie County sheriff Alfred "Smokey" Klaerner was making a turn onto one of those crazy streets in downtown San Antonio when an excited policeman came running toward the car, waving his arms and shouting, "Hey, mister, you can't make a left turn here." The sheriff, not wanting to contradict a fellow peace officer but considering himself a pretty fair judge of distance, calmly leaned out the window and said, "Yeah, I believe I can make it all right."

Alfred Klaerner was the Gillespie County sheriff from 1918 to 1920 and from 1924 to 1942. He is not to be confused with his brother John Klaerner, who was sheriff from 1900 to 1910, or his son Hugo Klaerner, who was sheriff from 1950 to 1980. Add that up and you'll see that a Klaerner was sheriff of Gillespie County for three-fifths of the twentieth century.

Central casting could not have turned up a more fitting symbol of law and order than Alfred Klaerner. He wore boots and a wide-brimmed hat with his badge pinned prominently to the lapel of his coat.

He was colorful and eccentric, and he played his role to the hilt. He rode his horse at the head of the Fourth of July Parade in Fredericksburg with a shotgun across his lap. Every so often along the parade route, he would raise his weapon in the air and blast away, providing his own fireworks.

Bill Petmecky described his friend Sheriff Klaerner as tough, fearless, practical and folksy. His quaint logic, mannerisms and speech were legendary all over South and West Texas.

Sheriff Alfred "Smokey" Klaerner. *Travis Klaerner.*

He operated in a different time and in ways that are no longer possible. As Bill Petmecky explained, "It may not have been legal to administer a few hard slaps to a wayward youngster, but it brought home some good lessons and saved the family from paying a fine for which the money might have to be deducted from the food bill."

More than once, Sheriff Klaerner poured out bootleg liquor rather than send the man to prison, which would have been hard on the family.

The 1920s and 1930s were precarious times for law enforcement. I could write of Sheriff Klaerner's wild car chases and shootouts, of which there were plenty, but I offer instead the story of Dan Hoerster's hat.

One day, while Dan Hoerster had lunch at the Ostrow Hotel in Fredericksburg (today's Fredericksburg Winery parking lot—old Knopp and Metzgers), someone stole his new Stetson. Hoerster marched straight to the sheriff's office, where an APB went out for the thief, who was believed to be headed east in a maroon car.

When Blanco County sheriff J.S. Casparis (another legendary character) stopped the car in Johnson City, Sheriff Klaerner hurried to Blanco County, searched the car, found the hat and brought the thief back to Fredericksburg, where Justice of the Peace Adolf Mergenthaler set the price for Stetson swiping at twenty-three dollars. The thief paid the fine and left town a poorer but wiser man.

In his off-duty hours, Sheriff Klaerner ran a store and a bar at Klaerner's Park, four miles out the Harper Road on Live Oak Creek (today's Lone Star Bar and Grill). He was a good singer. He played the fiddle and the cornet. He also conducted the Bunkusville Band.

Sheriff Klaerner was one of the founders of the Gillespie County Old Teamsters Reunion. He hosted many of the group's gatherings at Klaerner's Park.

He was tough as grandpa's toenails, but he had a sneaky sense of humor. His friend Ernst Zenner claimed Sheriff Klaerner originated the famous "blind horse" story.

The sheriff loved horses. He was especially fond of a dappled blue animal raised on his Live Oak Creek farm.

One day, a man who fancied himself an expert horse trader wanted to buy the animal, but Sheriff Klaerner refused, saying the horse "didn't look so good." The man was confused. "He looks all right to me," he said, but Sheriff Klaerner insisted again that the horse "didn't look so good." The man, growing impatient, said he wanted that horse no matter how he looked and offered the sheriff eighty dollars.

He bought himself a blind horse.

15

SALOONS

Symbols of Frontier Culture

T he first mark of civilization on the advancing western frontier was often a saloon. Frontiersmen built structures of lesser importance, like houses, churches and schools, as they got around to it.

Saloons were about more than just drinking. Saloons were gathering places. Drinking, after all, is best done in the company of others.

From 1860 to 1920, saloons dominated social life in small towns and big cities all over America. They were boisterous men's clubs where mostly working class menfolk with callused elbows and strong opinions debated politics and argued the important issues of the day.

Saloons and politics went together like coffee and the morning paper. Before some counties had courthouses or city halls, men conducted city and county business in saloons.

Saloons were democratic for their day. Every man (minorities excepted) was equal in a saloon—at least until the fight started. A thirsty patron checked his college degree and social status at the door before he bellied up to the rail to wet his whistle. A saloon was a beer drinker's republic where white men could passionately debate the issues on a more or less equal basis.

In 1897, there were an estimated 250,000 saloons in America. In today's terms, that's 20 saloons for every Starbucks.

In 1907, there were more saloons in Fredericksburg, Texas, than tourists. A lineup of drinking establishments scattered along San Saba Street, now Main Street, included the Buckhorn Saloon, the Bismarck Saloon, the Capital Saloon, the Crystal Saloon, Peter's Saloon, the White Elephant Saloon and the Bank Saloon.

The beer was as warm as sunshine and sold for a nickel a glass.

The décor of saloons often reflected local culture. Cow horns and buffalo hides decorated saloons on the plains. Moose horns dangled from the ceilings in saloons in Montana. The Texas Hill Country preferred deer horns.

Antlers covered the walls of the Buckhorn Saloon, one of the most popular watering holes in Fredericksburg. The Buckhorn occupied the lot where Security State Bank now stands.

Most saloons in Fredericksburg had pool tables and some form of gambling. In the early twentieth century, some Fredericksburg saloons had contraptions called "marble machines," an early form of slot machines. The White Elephant Saloon had a separate room out back where certain men played high-stakes poker.

Many horse races began with a liquored-up cowboy talking trash in a saloon. In Fredericksburg, the racetrack was the unpaved expanse of San Saba Street. The Nimitz Hotel was the starting line. The finish line was the front door of the Buckhorn Saloon. There winners celebrated, and losers drowned their sorrows.

By 1910, the saloons in Fredericksburg sold wines, liquors, cigars and all kinds of keg and bottled beers. A popular beer at the time was called Santone, bottled by the Lone Star Brewing Company of San Antonio.

When Texas blue laws ordered drinking establishments to close at midnight and on Sundays, saloons complied—sort of. The White Elephant Saloon always locked its front door at the appointed time, but the back door sometimes remained open all night and through weekend, especially if patrons were particularly numerous and thirsty or if a hot poker game was in progress.

Saloons were a way of life, and owning one was a perfectly respectable occupation. Herman Ochs, the owner of the Buckhorn Saloon, served as the Gillespie County sheriff from 1910 to 1918.

Saloons prospered until Prohibition wiped them out in 1919. Some historians insist that Prohibition was as much about politics as drinking. Prohibition, they say, was about the desire of the wealthy class to suppress the working man's vote by shutting down the places where political ideas formed and unions organized.

When the country repealed Prohibition in 1933, most people assumed the saloons would return. But saloons never made a comeback. They were from another time. They were too rowdy. They excluded women and minorities.

Drinking establishments slowly became more inclusive and more polite. They became bars, pubs, taverns, lounges, cantinas, breweries, beer gardens, ice houses and tasting rooms.

Saloons marked the beginning and the end of an era. They were the first imprint and the last bastion of America's frontier culture.

16

THE WHITE ELEPHANT SALOON

The White Elephant was hands down the most popular name for a drinking establishment in nineteenth-century Texas. There were White Elephant Saloons in Abilene, Austin, Brownsville, Brenham, Bryan, Denison, El Paso, Lampasas, Laredo, Mobeetie and Wichita Falls. The name was so familiar to Texans, it could have been a franchise.

The White Elephant Saloon in San Antonio was located on the north side of the Main Plaza, near San Fernando Church. At the White Elephant Saloon in Fort Worth, gunfighter Luke Short got crossways with Longhaired Jim Courtright. Short drew first and gave Courtright the longest funeral procession the city of Fort Worth had ever seen. That was the long and short of it.

The White Elephant Saloon at 242 East Main Street in Fredericksburg may have been the classiest joint of any saloon in Texas that carried the name. John Kleck built it in 1888. Its exterior walls were cut limestone with three double doors in front and an ornamental wrought iron railing along the top. Until 1938, there was a wooden gallery out front.

Inside the building, the long wooden bar was along the west wall. There was a large mirror on the back wall with an ice chest underneath to keep the beer kegs cold. There was a cistern under the floor near the front of the building.

Carbide lights lit up the bar at night. Later, workers installed electric lights when Pfeil's power plant made electricity available.

To put the finishing touch on the front of his fancy saloon, John Kleck hired two stonemasons, A.W. Petmecky and a man named Thompson,

White Elephant Saloon, 242 East Main Street, Fredericksburg. *Author's photograph.*

to carve or mold an elephant and attach it to the outside wall above the middle door.

That assignment proved to be a tall order. Images of elephants were hard to find in the Texas Hill Country.

As luck would have it, there was, at the time, a merry-go-'round on Marketplatz operated by a gentleman from Italy. For a small fee, children could ride around in a circle on the backs of wooden animals from around the world. One of the animals was an elephant.

Petmecky and Thompson got permission to make an imprint of the elephant by removing it from the merry-go-'round and pressing it into a large container of moist sand. Then they poured cement containing lime into the imprint to form the elephant we see today.

In 1893, John Kleck leased the building to saloonkeepers John Klaerner and Henry Langerhans for twenty-five dollars a month, but there was an interesting provision in the lease that allowed Kleck to terminate the agreement if the railroad came to town.

Klaerner and Langerhans bought the contents of the saloon for $1,400—$400 in cash and a $1,000 loan. Business was good. They paid off the loan in less than a year.

The White Elephant Saloon served the men of Fredericksburg until Prohibition. Over the next fifty years, the building housed a tractor and farm implement company, a grocery store, a barbershop and a dealership for Hudson-Essex automobiles.

The origin of the name White Elephant comes from Southeast Asian culture. White elephants were sacred in that part of the world. They were pampered and did no work of any kind. By the time the term arrived in America, it had come to mean—sometimes in a tongue in cheek sort of way—an expensive but worthless investment.

The name White Elephant may also relate to the phrase "seeing the elephant," a nineteenth-century expression that referred to a great adventure.

Some sources in Fredericksburg say the name came from a custom in parts of Germany in which a white elephant was a symbol for an eating and drinking establishment.

Because frontier saloons were segregated, the name also had racial overtones. There were Black Elephant Saloons in Fort Worth, Brenham, Austin, Houston and San Antonio that catered to Black Americans.

Saloons thrived in Texas until Prohibition hit the booze industry like a herd of elephants.

When the White Elephant Saloon in San Antonio closed, a local newspaper wrote with a noticeable tone of sadness, "When the boys come to San Antone, they can't milk the elephant anymore."

17

LAST DANCE AT PAT'S HALL

Pat's Hall in Fredericksburg was not an easy place to find. It was off the beaten path, hidden away on the edge of town, down a narrow, winding road and across the creek.

But country music fans from all over the Hill Country managed to find it every Saturday night. Pat's Hall was a hub of weekend entertainment and a showcase for aspiring country music artists for thirty years.

Pat's Hall was different from the traditional wooden dance halls in Luckenbach, Hye, Albert and Sisterdale. Pat's Hall had masonry walls and real glass windows. The building didn't lean, droop or sag.

Pat's Hall had two dance floors. There was an inside floor and an outdoor pavilion where couples could two-step, waltz, schottische and cotton-eyed joe, weather permitting, on the circular dance floor around a big oak tree.

There was nothing quite like dancing in the moonlight to good country music, with the stars twinkling through the oak leaves.

Pat's Hall opened in the 1920s as Seipp's Hall. Then J.J. Patranella bought the place in the early 1950s and changed the name to Pat's Hall. For the next thirty years, Pat's Hall hosted local and regional acts, rising stars and country music legends.

Back in the horse and buggy days, Texas dance halls were hubs for social activity in German communities throughout the Hill Country. After World War II, rural dance halls, like Pat's Hall, became proving grounds for future stars of American popular music.

Smiley Whitley was one of the early stars to play at Pat's Hall. Smiley played a triple-necked Fender steel guitar and fronted a ten-piece western swing band.

Pat's Hall, Fredericksburg. *Author's photograph.*

Sonny Burns was another popular performer in the early 1950s. Sonny was a talented honky-tonk artist and a friend of George Jones. Unfortunately, Sonny shared many of George's bad habits.

The Rolling Stones played Pat's Hall on August 7, 1954—no, not the legendary English rock group but an Austin-based rockabilly band fronted by singer Leon Carter.

Most of the men and women who played Pat's Hall week in and week out were hardworking troubadours who toiled on the Texas dance hall circuit. They had weekday jobs and played music on weekends. They had strong regional followings, and many of them made records, but they never gained the popularity to make it big. Those artists included Jimmy Heap, Bubba Littrell, George Chambers, the Moods of Country Music, the Debonaires, Clifton Jansky, Adolph Hofner, Fiddlin' Phil Trimble, the Rounders, the Metheny Brothers and the Circle C Band.

Occasionally, a performer on the dance hall circuit would break out and become a star on the radio and the *Grand Ole Opry*.

A short list of stars who performed at Pat's Hall included Jack Greene, Johnny Bush, Moe Bandy, Charlie Walker, Hank Thompson, Kenny Price (from the television show *Hee Haw*), Wanda Jackson, Fiddlin' Frenchie Burke and Bill Mack, a country singer and songwriter best known as the Midnight Cowboy on Radio Station WBAP in Fort Worth.

On rare nights, Pat's Hall hosted legends. Willie Nelson played Pat's Hall on June 8, 1968. George Strait and the Ace in the Hole Band took the stage on October 22, 1976.

While music and dancing were always front and center, Pat's Hall offered a variety of entertainment. Pat's sometimes hosted wrestling matches. The baseball diamond behind the dance hall was home to the Fredericksburg Giants of the Hill Country League. Local high school teams played there, too.

But with each passing year, Pat's Hall had a harder time paying the bills. The cost of doing business rose. Profit margins shrank. Dance halls had a hard time competing with television. Bands demanded more of the gate. Insurance rates climbed. Beverage tax rates increased.

Texas dance halls fell victim to shifting demographics. Most dance halls were located in small towns. Rural working-class patrons were always the backbone of the business. As Texas became a more urban state, the popularity of dance halls declined.

Johnny Paycheck played the final night at Pat's Hall in June 1985. After that, another Texas dance hall shut the door and turned out the lights.

The party was over.

18

Peter's Hall

When Ed Peter built a large wooden dance hall behind his saloon and restaurant in Fredericksburg, it quickly became an important part of community life. Peter's Hall was a gathering place for people of all ages and an amusement center unlike any other.

In 1903, Ed Peter and Herman Mosel opened a saloon and restaurant in a stone building on the corner of Main and Orange Streets. One year later, Peter bought out Mosel and became the sole proprietor.

Carpenters built the large wooden hall behind the saloon in 1910. A breezeway connected the two buildings.

Peter's Hall, with its large open floor space, was a dance hall and more. It was an all-purpose community center that served a multitude of functions.

In the early days of silent films, Peter's Hall helped introduce Fredericksburg to Fatty Arbuckle, Charlie Chaplin, Buster Keaton, Harold Lloyd, William S. Hart and Pearl White.

Anticipating Prohibition, Ed Peter bought a soda fountain from Hanisch and Payne Drug Store in Fredericksburg. Throughout the 1920s and early 1930s, Peter's sold fountain drinks, candy and near beer.

Traveling vaudeville shows performed at Peter's Hall in the early twentieth century. Vaudeville, a collection of diverse specialty acts featuring singers, dancers, jugglers, acrobats and comedians, was a popular form of live entertainment until the movies put it out of business.

Of the vaudevillians who entertained audiences at Peter's Hall, a few were truly talented. Most, like Murphy the acting monkey and the guy who played the flute with his nose, were simply quirky.

Peter's Hall, Fredericksburg. *Gillespie County Historical Society.*

Peter's Hall also hosted wrestling matches and music recitals. Its massive wooden floor converted to a skating rink. Fredericksburg High School played home basketball games there in the 1920s and 1930s. Fredericksburg High School and St. Mary's High School held graduation ceremonies there.

On February 13, 1928, the J.I. Case Company gave an exhibition of its new threshing machine at Peter's Hall. Beginning in the 1930s the local Chevrolet dealer announced its new models at Peter's Hall.

The Louis Jordan Post of the American Legion was founded in Peter's Hall. Officials of the Hill Country Baseball League often met at Peter's Hall to plan the coming season.

For years, Peter's Hall was the site of the Miss Fredericksburg Pageant. The Fredericksburg Garden Club held its annual flower show there. Fredericksburg Publishing Co., the gas company and local appliance dealers sponsored a yearly cooking school at Peter's Hall.

Peter's Hall was also one of the twenty-three polling places in Gillespie County. Election night at Peter's was a huge event, especially during presidential election years. People from all over the county gathered to watch the votes tallied on a big chalk board.

Perhaps the most spectacular events held at Peter's Hall were the singing festivals.

Following a tradition brought from Germany, towns throughout the German Hill Country formed singing clubs. Peter's Hall often hosted the Gillespie County Singing Festival and the regional singing festival whenever it came to Fredericksburg.

The regional festival began at ten o'clock on a Saturday morning with a parade of participants down Main Street. The parade began at the

Nimitz Hotel and ended at Peter's Hall. There, the parade disbanded for "refreshments, songs and rehearsals."

Groups performed for bragging rights. No sporting event was more hotly contested. The highlight of the weekend was a mass chorus, often over six hundred voices strong, performing for a capacity crowd at Peter's Hall.

The heyday of Peter's Hall came in the time before television. People spent leisure hours with friends and neighbors, eating, drinking, dancing, singing and socializing.

Soldiers returning from World War II stopped at home and then went to Peter's Hall for a beer.

Then in the 1950s, business at Peter's Hall declined. Television changed entertainment habits and social patterns. People stayed home more, watching *I Love Lucy* and eating TV dinners. Peter's Hall was from another time, and its time had passed.

By 1960, the old wooden building was in need of repair, but the owners decided to sell the property, which sat on prime Main Street real estate, rather than repair the hall and keep the business going.

Workers razed Peter's Hall in 1960 to make way for the Community Savings and Loan building, now Fredericksburg PNC Bank.

19

VAUDEVILLE

It's Not Just a Naughty French Word

Mr. and Mrs. Poole were an ordinary couple from Illinois, except that every night, before a cheering crowd, she threw knives at his head, and he shot pieces of chalk from her ears. Their vaudeville routine followed a troupe of one-legged acrobats and a pair of boxing monkeys.

Vaudeville comprised fast-paced variety shows featuring a series of live acts. It was a popular form of entertainment in America in the late nineteenth and early twentieth centuries, especially in cities. Many rural folk were reluctant to accept vaudeville at first.

The word *vaudeville* is French and may be a mispronunciation of Vau-de-Vire, an area of northern France known for its bawdy drinking songs. It was those French origins that made many rural Texans suspicious of vaudeville.

The French had a reputation for immodesty. To Texans, even polite French words sounded naughty.

To make matters worse, some people confused vaudeville with burlesque, which was a more provocative style of adult entertainment, often with sexual overtones. Burlesque, from an Italian word meaning to joke, mock or ridicule, was vaudeville's dirty little brother.

For these and other reasons, vaudeville didn't always have the best reputation, especially in the more conservative parts of the country.

In 1884, a San Antonio newspaper described the city's vaudeville dens as "a blot on civilization," especially after assassins killed gunfighters Ben Thompson and King Fisher in a wild shootout at Jack Harris's Vaudeville Theater, "a vile place fronting San Antonio's Main Plaza."

Vaudeville even had a less than sterling reputation in show business circles. Serious thespians coined the term "legitimate theater" to separate themselves from the low-class beerhall singers, can-can dancers and medicine show barkers who were the original vaudeville performers.

But once vaudeville caught on in the countryside, people couldn't get enough of it. Klaerner's Opera House, Peter's Hall and the Palace Theater in Fredericksburg hosted regular vaudeville shows. So did the Arcadia Theater and Pampell's Opera House in Kerrville.

Other shows performed in tents. In January 1923, the Grandi Brothers Stock Company came to Fredericksburg, set up a tent at Marktplatz and stayed a week. Advertisements claimed the tent was "double walled, as warm and cozy as your living room and absolutely waterproof."

The cost for a ticket was forty cents for adults and ten cents for children.

Knowing the conservative nature of rural Texas communities, managers were careful to stage shows that were "strictly clean and moral." The style came to be called "polite vaudeville."

At the same time, theater managers carefully screened new acts. They sent "impolite" scripts back to actors in blue envelopes, leading to the phrase "blue material," a reference to content that was too hot to handle.

It is interesting to note that just about every act that passed through the Hill Country in those days had "recently returned from a tour of Europe, where the cast entertained the crowned heads of state." Singers and dancers were "fresh from the Broadway stage."

Of course, there was no way to check the validity of those claims. The internet hadn't been invented yet.

The typical "polite" vaudeville shows featured singers, dancers and comedians, in addition to all kinds of interesting specialty acts.

An early vaudeville show at Peter's Hall in Fredericksburg starred Baby Edna, a world champion child buck and wing dancer.

Another show featured Lady Pat, a horse who could add, subtract, multiply and divide. Lady Pat could also tell time, and she could pick out the flags of different countries.

Some vaudeville shows staged boxing and wrestling matches. Dancers performed serpentine dancing, also called skirt dancing, a toned-down version of the can-can. Monologists recited Shakespeare and *Casey at the Bat*.

But there was trouble ahead for vaudeville. Radio hurt ticket sales in the 1920s. Then an exciting new form of entertainment knocked Vaudeville for a loop.

In 1927, talking pictures took the country by storm. By 1935, most vaudeville theaters had been converted to movie houses, and the top talent had left vaudeville for radio and Hollywood.

But in its heyday, vaudeville was the theater of the people. It had something for everybody. It was the most democratic art form in American history.

20

Marking Time at
the Palace Theatre

The Palace Theatre marked time in Fredericksburg for most of the twentieth century. The grand old movie house was a part of the fabric of the community.

In 1926, John Stahl, the operator of the Palace Theatre in New Braunfels, purchased Klaerner's Opera House, Dance Hall and Confectionary on Main Street in Fredericksburg. The new owner brought in chairs and a screen and converted the opera house into a movie theatre.

One of the earliest films shown at Stahl's Palace Theatre in Fredericksburg was a Harold Lloyd silent comedy called *Hot Water*, but two-reel westerns, called "oaters," were crowd favorites. Early westerns shown at the Palace included *The Flying Horseman*, starring Buck Jones; *Man in the Saddle*, starring Hoot Gibson, Faye Wray and Boris Karloff; and *Somewhere in Sonora*, starring Ken Maynard.

In 1928, Stahl announced plans to build a new Palace Theatre on the site of the old one. Demolition began in the summer of 1929. During construction, Stahl showed his movies in a rented building on Llano Street.

The new theater opened on December 23, 1929, four weeks after the stock market crash. The building, with an Art Deco–style front, had the latest bells and whistles, including a Movietone projection system. Movietone was a technique that recorded sound directly onto film, ensuring that the moving pictures and sound were always in sync. Equipped with Movietone, the Palace could show 'talkies" although many people believed talking pictures were a fad that wouldn't last.

Palace Theater, 142 East Main Street, Fredericksburg. *Author's photograph.*

The first film shown at the new Palace was *Sweetie*, a talkie starring Jack Oakey and Helen Kane, the "Boop-Boop-a-Doop" girl.

In the 1930s and 1940s many children in Fredericksburg belonged to the Popeye Club, named after the cartoon character Popeye the sailor. Members could see a movie, usually starring Shirley Temple, every Saturday morning for ten cents.

The Palace presented live performances as well as movies. On January 28, 1930, legendary singer Jimmy Rodgers played the Palace. In the summer of 1948, the Palace hosted the Hill Country Jamboree, broadcast live on KNAF 1340. The acts included the Texas Tune Wranglers, the Singing Waiters and the Nebgen Sisters. On December 10, 1963, the Palace hosted a live folk music show called a hootenanny, sponsored by the Jaycees, with proceeds going to help needy children at Christmas. Several acts canceled, including the Red River Ramblers and the Night Riders, citing the recent assassination of President Kennedy.

Country singer and actor Marty Robbins chose the Palace as the site for the state premier of his movie *Ballad of a Gunfighter* on September 6, 1963.

For years, city officials announced the winner of the First Baby of the Year contest from the stage at the Palace. It seems the tradition started in March 1928, when the Palace began showing photographs of local newborn babies on the big screen. The audience voted on the cutest baby. First prize was five dollars in gold.

Over the years, the Palace hosted community events, town meetings and concerts. The Palace was a precinct polling place for city, county, state and national elections.

You could witness the changing tastes of America through the kind of movies shown at the Palace. Abbott and Costello, westerns and Disney's animated movies dominated the 1950s. The Three Stooges, Jerry Lewis, Elvis Presley, James Bond and beach movies were popular in the early 1960s.

In the late 1960s, Hollywood began making movies with more provocative content. Fredericksburg wasn't always comfortable with the trend.

On May 18, 1971, local law enforcement officers confiscated the movie, *No Blade of Grass*, which had been shown the night before at the Palace, after parents complained of its language and risqué subject matter.

But parents didn't worry too much. Most movies shown at the Palace were squeaky clean.

Over time, people in Fredericksburg forged lifelong relationships at the Palace. Couples went to the Palace on their first dates. Parents took their children. Grandparents took grandchildren.

Then in 2000 changing economics caused the Palace to close. The building, in the heart of Fredericksburg's business district, was more valuable as a retail store than a movie theater.

Now, there is a new movie house in town with a wine bar, seats as comfortable as my recliner, rip-roaring audio-visuals and other amazing amenities.

I have good memories of the Palace, although I wonder how I was able to sit through a whole movie without a glass of wine.

21

HOODWINKED BY HOLLYWOOD

T he people of Fredericksburg and Gillespie County were thrilled when they heard that Hollywood was coming to make a movie in the spring of 1970. Their hill country home was among the most picturesque places on Earth. It was high time the rest of the world found out about it.

Producer-director Larry Buchanan chose Gillespie County for his film, *Strawberries Need Rain*, because the German Hill Country looked like Sweden. Buchanan was a fan of iconic Swedish filmmaker Ingmar Bergman.

Buchanan milked the Bergman connection for all it was worth. *Texas Monthly Magazine* called *Strawberries Need Rain* a "sensitive Bergmanesque drama." Buchanan allegedly talked some Dallas theater owners into advertising the movie as a Bergman film in the hopes that more people would see it.

Of course, many Texans, myself included, didn't share Hollywood's fascination with Ingmar Bergman. If John Wayne's not in it, I'm not interested.

Larry Buchanan was known for writing, producing and directing low-budget blockbusters, like *It's Alive* (under the name Larry Cohen) and *Creatures of Destruction*. He made many films for less than $30,000, far less than the cost of a modern-day thirty-second TV commercial.

The cast and crew of *Strawberries Need Rain* arrived in Fredericksburg on April 4, 1970. The biggest star of the movie was Les Tremayne, a well-respected English radio and movie actor who previously had roles in *The Fortune Cookie*, *Girl Happy* with Elvis Presley and Alfred Hitchcock's *North by Northwest.*

By the next afternoon, the crew had transformed the area behind the Gillespie County Courthouse into a movie set. As cameras rolled, Felix Pehl's Old Time Band played music on the gazebo. Extras included members of the community theater group and fourteen Mormon missionaries who were passing through town. Even people walking down the street got caught up in the hoopla.

The crew filmed other scenes at the Pioneer Museum, Vereins Kirche, Cross Mountain, City Cemetery, Doss and Lange's Mill. Doss students and teachers appeared as extras.

Les Tremayne played the grim reaper. Actress Monica Gayle played a young girl with one day to live.

Trailers described it as "a sensitive, sensual film." As for the plot, let's just say the word *sensual* should have been a red flag and leave it at that.

Strawberries Need Rain opened at the Palace Theater in Fredericksburg on February 4, 1973. Opening night was a sellout.

The crowd cheered when the movie began, but the excitement faded fast. Just about everyone agreed it was an awful picture. The script was sophomoric. The acting was terrible. Once critic said Les Tremayne looked "tired and embarrassing."

The *Fredericksburg Standard* pulled no punches. "*Strawberries Need Rain* Not Worth Seeing," read the headline. The only good thing about the movie was its scenery. The actors looked and acted like they "had been picked up on a street corner."

But the nude scenes were what shocked viewers. Fredericksburg felt betrayed, hoodwinked by Hollywood.

The *Fredericksburg Standard* described the "pornographic scenes" in the R-rated film as some of the "rankest ever seen by many locals." Reactions from moviegoers ranged from "anger to outrage."

Fredericksburg learned a tough lesson. The town would ask a lot more questions next time.

"We have an idea," said an article in the *Standard*, "that the next group of movie-making folks that come to Fredericksburg will not receive the same type of cooperation extended the group that filmed this one."

The film did spark an interesting debate. Many citizens expressed a belief that nude scenes in movies lead to promiscuous behavior, while others noted that the same folks who complained about nudity had no objections to horrific depictions of violence and bloodshed on the big screen.

One young man from Fredericksburg wrote, "I believe it is a sad reflection on the values in our society when an occasional 'R'-rated movie is frowned upon and scandalized, while a host of bloody epics go unannounced at the Saturday matinee."

Something to think about it light of recent events.

22

MAKING OUT AT THE 87 DRIVE-IN

Going to a movie at a modern indoor theater is all about the movie. Going to a movie at the drive-in was about girls, hanging out with friends and showing off your new set of mud grips. If you actually watched Randolph Scott plug the bad guy and then give the schoolmarm a kiss that could water a horse, so much the better.

The drive-in was about the people and the atmosphere. The movie was often incidental.

Even if the movie was a stinker, it was better to go to the drive-in than stay home and watch the two snowy channels on your black-and-white TV set. You even had to get off the couch to change the channel.

The American drive-in movie craze began in the 1930s. A whole culture grew up around it.

The drive-in was a community event for all ages. Children played on the swings in front of the giant screen. Older folks set up folding chairs in front of their cars or parked their pickups backward and sat on chairs in the bed. Some families brought sleeping bags for the kids.

You could bring your own food and beverages. The drive-in was the original dinner and a movie.

Early arrivals got the preferred spots—front and center if they wanted to watch the movie or the back row if they had other things in mind.

Time slowed down at the drive-in. There was no rigid schedule. Starting times varied with the seasons. The projectionist had to wait for Mother Nature to turn down the house lights. The show began at dusk, whenever that was.

87 Drive-In, Fredericksburg. *Gillespie County Historical Society.*

Most of all, the drive-in was about freedom. Parents weren't around. Viewers were outdoors, and they weren't confined to a seat. They didn't have to shut up for two hours. They could walk around, annoy people in the other cars and even toss a Frisbee with a friend.

Fredericksburg's drive-in was the 87 Drive-In Theater. It sat in a field next to a peach orchard on what is now a vacant lot on the corner of Highway 87 and Friendship Lane.

The 87 Drive-In opened to great fanfare on June 11, 1949. I don't know the name of the movie that played that first night, but one of the early films shown at the 87 Drive-In was the *The Kissing Bandit*, starring Frank Sinatra. I've been told by people who were there that the kissing on the screen was a drop in the bucket compared to the lip action occurring in the audience.

There was a reason drive-ins were called passion pits.

The 87 Drive-In had spaces for three hundred cars. The original screen was fifty by fifty feet. There was a recreational area for kids up front and seating space for adults, all surrounded by a seven-foot-tall fence.

A night at the 87 Drive-In was a bargain; it cost two dollars a head to get in, and that didn't count the number of friends you could stuff in the trunk. Children under the age of twelve got in for free. On certain nights, the price of admission was five dollars a carload.

Often, on weekends, the 87 Drive-In showed a double feature. Connoisseurs of fine cinema could see *Beach Blanket Bingo* and *I was a Teenage Werewolf* for the price of one ticket.

It's been a long time since I've been to a drive-in, but I had an experience a while back that reminded me how much fun watching a film under the stars, both celestial and cinematic, could be. On a trip to San Antonio, my wife and I saw John Wayne's *The Alamo* in Alamo Plaza in front of the Alamo. It was unforgettable.

In the 1950s, at the peak of drive-in mania, there were about four thousand drive-ins across the country. Then cable television, VCRs and DVDs put most drive-ins out of business.

Land prices in cities skyrocketed, causing developers to swap drive-ins for strip malls.

For most of us, a night at the drive-in was part of an era that vanished from the American landscape.

Fredericksburg's 87 Drive-In is long gone, but there are about four hundred drive-ins across the country that are still in business.

Drive-ins are not extinct, but they are on the endangered species list.

23

THE DOMINO PARLOR

I didn't know *willkommen* from *auf wiedersehen* the first time I wandered into the Domino Parlor in Fredericksburg. It was the summer of 1981. I was the new guy in town, looking for a fast game of Moon or 42, but there wasn't a domino in sight.

The Domino Parlor that many of us remember is the impressive rectangular building with the cut limestone walls, multiple front doors and distinctive bay window. It stands just east of what used to be Dietz Bakery on Main Street. The building is about 160 years old, although its earliest history is a little uncertain.

The German Emigration Company originally assigned the town lot at what is now 222 East Main Street to Adolph Schildknecht but deeded it to Schildknecht's assignee John Schmidtzinsky in 1849. A fire destroyed the original deed in 1850.

Schmidtzinsky then sold the property to J.A. Alberthal in 1858. The building we now know as the Domino Parlor probably existed then, because the purchase price of $500 seemed to indicate there was a building on the property. Elise Kowert wrote in the *Fredericksburg Standard*, "In all probability, John Schmidtzinsky built the front part of the house."

J.A. Alberthal and his family likely lived in the building while he ran a saloon. When the place sold again several years later, a notation in the deed referred to a "dwelling house and a small space between the same and the house adjoining the same on lot 176 known as Alberthal's bar room."

Domino Parlor (the one-story building in the middle), 222 East Main Street, Fredericksburg. *Gillespie County Historical Society.*

A little known but fascinating feature of the building is its large cellar with a domed rock ceiling. The builder filled the cellar with a dome of sand to hold the ceiling in place until the mortar dried.

The hermit Peter Berg probably built the cellar. He built one at the Keidel House just down the street. Because the cellars at the Keidel House and the old Domino Parlor are so similar, many people believe Berg built them both.

In 1860, J.A. Alberthal sold the building to Ottocar Mueller and Christian Frantzen for $1,100. Mueller and Frantzen operated a drugstore there. When Frantzen died, Mueller became the sole owner.

Ottocar Mueller sold the property to Adolph Dreiss in 1873. Max von Reinbach lived there for a time and operated a drugstore in the front room.

Henry Richter, born in Baltimore and raised in Virginia, bought the building in 1901. Richter lived in the back of the building with his wife and children and sold jewelry and musical instruments out of the front room. The bay window was Richter's show window.

Richter was an interesting character. He was a cultured man and very musical. He played the violin, classical guitar and several other instruments. He was also a composer. He knew and corresponded with Antonin Dvorak, one of the first Czech composers to achieve worldwide recognition.

Henry Richter was also a member of the local Casino Club. He promoted the masked ball and organized the Philharmonische Geschellschaft (philharmonic society), which included a mixed choir and orchestra. The society presented concerts in the large front room, and the music spilled out onto Main Street. What a thrill it must have been to hear the music as it drifted in and out of the open doors and windows all over Fredericksburg.

In 1945, the Richter heirs sold the building to Walter Knoche. Over the next twenty-eight years, the old building housed a Mexican food restaurant, a pool hall and a domino parlor.

When William Wareing bought the property from Elsie Knoche in 1973, the Domino Parlor was rundown and in need of some serious attention. So, Wareing removed the old plaster, repointed the rock work and returned the building to its original appearance. He took out the dominoes and the pool table and opened a sandwich shop and beer garden.

I visited the old Domino Parlor (now Grandma Daisy's) recently just to look around. It looked a lot different than I remembered, but one thing hasn't changed.

Not a domino was in the place.

24

THE TOWER

Do you ever wonder how teenagers kept up with each other in the days before cellphones and instant communication? If you were a teenager in Fredericksburg in the 1960s and 1970s, cruising Main Street on Saturday night, you would make a swing through the parking lot of the Tower Drive-In. Everyone showed up there sooner or later. It was the best show in town.

The Tower, at 526 West Main Street, shared a low-slung, flat-roofed building with Jim's Ice House at the corner of Bowie and Main Streets (where Jek's Pit Stop is today). The business got its name from the big water tower just up the street. Newspaper advertisements called the Tower "the most popular drive-in in town," and for a time, it was, especially with teenagers who were itching to get out from under their parents' thumbs.

The Tower's busy kitchen served hamburgers, chicken, shrimp and the restaurant's famous finger steaks, while the soda fountain cranked out malts, milkshakes, banana splits and soft serve ice cream.

The Tower offered inside dining, curbside service and food to-go. Carhops took orders and carried food to curbside customers on metal trays that hung on car doors. The food was good, and the price was reasonable. There was a time when hungry teenagers on a budget could buy a hamburger, fries and a drink for forty-nine cents.

But the Tower was much more than a restaurant. It was a part of the American drive-in culture created by teenagers who were looking for something to do on Saturday night.

The Tower Restaurant, Fredericksburg. *Gillespie County Historical Society.*

Teenagers want to be independent, and in the 1960s and 1970s, independence meant getting behind the wheel. A car meant freedom. A driver's license marked the transition to adulthood.

By the 1960s, most families had cars, often more than one. Gasoline cost twenty cents a gallon. The call of the open road was irresistible.

In towns all over America, cruising became a weekend ritual (adults called it "driving around aimlessly"). In Fredericksburg, it was no trick at all to put fifty miles on the family Chevy in one night, just cruising (some called it dragging) Main Street, back and forth, between the "Y" (where the highway forks north of town) and the Nimitz Hotel, all on a dollar's worth of gas. Part of the routine included a stop at the Tower to see if anything interesting was going on—as if anyone had to ask.

There, in the Tower parking lot, teens hung out with friends (adults called it "loitering"), listened to music and did what fun-loving teenagers do best: strut, swagger and show off.

Squealing tires, booming radios and loud exhaust pipes were part of the charm of the Tower. Out in the parking lot, there was more action than a three-ring circus. Sparks flew as sweethearts got together and broke up, sometimes on the same night. There was plenty of laughter, theatrics, trash talk and an occasional fistfight. Every Friday and Saturday night, the curtain went up on a new production, sometimes a comedy, sometimes a drama and sometimes musical.

Car radios, eight-track tape players and the Tower's exterior speakers playing songs from the Wurlitzer jukebox in the dining room provided the soundtrack, except on certain Saturdays in the fall when most everyone tuned in to hear the Texas Longhorns and local legend Happy Feller play football. Even Aggies cheered when Happy booted one through the uprights.

Few patrons, even the hardcore regulars, knew what it took to run a place like the Tower. The hours were long and grueling—8:00 a.m. to midnight, Monday through Thursday, with special late hours on Friday and Saturday.

Tommy and Polly Zenner ran the Tower from 1967 to 1974. "On Saturday nights, when Pat's Hall was open, we didn't close until 2:00 a.m.," Polly told me. "After cleanup, we took the employees home. Sometimes, we didn't get home until 4:00 a.m."

As the setting sun cast long shadows on Sunday evening, the Tower parking lot was mostly empty and strangely silent, as if it was resting up for the next curtain call, when the chaos, comedy and drama would start all over again.

25

SUNNY SIDE HUT

Walter and Mary Hollmig probably didn't know they were shaping American culture when they opened Sunny Side Hut at 204 West Main Street in Fredericksburg. They were just trying to sell a few hamburgers.

At first glance, the year 1933 may not seem like an ideal time to start a business. The Great Depression had just hit small town America right in the gut. Both Fredericksburg banks had defaulted in 1932. The economy was a mess. Money was scarce.

But the Hollmigs believed better times were just around the corner, so they opened a restaurant in the middle of the worst financial crisis in history. To survive, they learned to be thrifty and creative in attracting customers.

Mary Hollmig named the business Sunny Side Hut. The name expressed her optimism and cheery disposition.

Walter and Mary's business model took advantage of three trends in American society: the end of Prohibition, the country's growing fondness for convenience food and Americans' love affair with the automobile.

At least two large businesses were already catering to Americans' affection for automobiles and fast food. National restaurant chains A&W and the Pig Stand delivered burgers, sandwiches and fries to customers who preferred to eat in their cars. Both companies claimed to be the first to use carhops (a variation of a bellhop) since the 1920s.

Walter and Mary Hollmig were travelers. It is likely they saw the drive-in concept during one of their journeys and brought it back to the Texas Hill Country.

The original Sunny Side Hut, a small wooden building where Broadway Bank stands today, had no indoor dining. Customers either walked or drove up and ordered through the window. Then, in 1941, the Hollmigs added on to the building, providing space for a small indoor dining area, restrooms and storage. Sometime in the evolutionary process, Walter and Mary hired carhops for the convenience of the drive-up customers.

After World War II the dining area had a few tables, a Wurlitzer jukebox and a Skee-Ball game. Adults played dominoes in the back of the building by the walk-in cooler.

But drive-up customers were the heart of the business. Cars would pull up in front of the building in the shade of a large canvas awning. Carhops would take orders and deliver the food to the driver in his car.

Sunny Side Hut served what has become standard fast-food fare, including burgers, fries, hot dogs, sandwiches, enchiladas, fountain drinks and ice cream. Walter Hollmig created the restaurant's ice cream in a room in the back of the building that today houses the Nevins Law Firm. Sunny Side Hut offered a variation of a Coney Island hot dog after Mary Hollmig had a Coney for lunch on a trip to New York.

Sunny Side Hut, Fredericksburg. *Gillespie County Historical Society.*

In addition to standard fast-food fare, the kitchen turned out a mean T-bone steak, and the bar served ice-cold beer on tap or in a bottle.

Sunny Side Hut was ahead of the curve in other ways. Customers could phone in their orders and have their food delivered to their homes or businesses free of charge.

Walter and Mary treated their employees like family. Every night after work, the Hollmigs drove the carhops home in the Walter's baby blue Lincoln Continental.

Until it closed in 1961, Sunny Side Hut was an important hub of community life in Fredericksburg. Teenagers gathered there after home football games, dances and movies. Teens were always welcome at Sunny Side, although there was that annoying adolescent fad of stealing salt and pepper shakers. Parents took younger children there to celebrate special events and as bribery for good behavior. If children showed good manners at church or at Oma's house, their parents took them to Sunny Side Hut for ice cream.

Sunny Side Hut was a cool oasis on a hot Texas day in a time when air conditioning was just catching on. "The frosty root beer at Sunny Side was sugar sweet and ice cold," a former Fredericksburg teenager told me. "And the beer was the coldest in town."

26

STANDING IN LINE
AT DIETZ BAKERY

T here was a time when the line of people that stretched down the Fredericksburg sidewalk in the early morning hours could only mean a couple of things: (1) the Texas Lottery reached $100 million, or (2) Dietz Bakery was open.

Dietz Bakery was a Fredericksburg institution. It had a reputation for having some of the best bread that ever got on the outside of a Reuben sandwich.

The bakery that came to be called Dietz was started in 1924, when Martin Schult opened a bakery in the Wahrmund building at 312 East Main Street (today Der Lindenbaum). In 1929, Schult sold the business to William Moellendorf, who had bakery experience in Gonzales, Luling and San Antonio. In 1939, Moellendorf sold out to his brother-in-law Theo Dietz.

The Dietz family ran the bakery for the next seventy years. Theo, born in Gillespie County in 1880, was an experienced baker, having operated bakeries in Kerrville and Kingsville. In 1954, Theo's son Edgar, a flour salesman, took over the business. When Edgar retired, his son Don ran the bakery.

In 1965 Dietz Bakery moved up the street to 214 East Main Street, next door to the Domino Parlor.

The workday at Dietz began at 2:00 a.m., when the early birds began sifting flour to a velvety smoothness. Dietz used flour from Pioneer Mills in San Antonio, a company with roots in Fredericksburg.

Dietz Bakery, 221 East Main Street, Fredericksburg. *Gillespie County Historical Society.*

Bakers then blended the ingredients in a large mixer. The mixed dough fermented for two hours before skilled hands weighed it and kneaded it on a long counter dusted with flour. Next, workers molded the dough and placed it in baking pans.

Before going into the oven, the molded dough sat in a rectangular wooden container called a "proof box." The steam from a kettle of hot water in the bottom of the proof box moistened the dough and caused it to rise. As soon as the dough rose to the proper height, bakers placed the containers in a gas-fired oven.

The bakery sold many of the finished loaves over the counter. The rest went to local grocery stores and restaurants.

Dietz Bakery made white bread, French loaf, rye, whole wheat and pumpernickel. A local favorite was a white loaf known as a "pull-apart." It comprised two loaves that were baked together then pulled apart, leaving a crusty "heel" at one end of each loaf.

The white bread had a chewy golden crust and was soft on the inside. The pumpernickel, made from coarsely ground rye berries, was dark and hearty.

On many Fridays and Saturdays and before special holidays, Dietz Bakery rose to the occasion and baked two batches. The second batch often hit the shelves before noon.

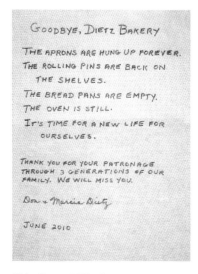

GOODBYE, DIETZ BAKERY

THE APRONS ARE HUNG UP FOREVER.
THE ROLLING PINS ARE BACK ON
    THE SHELVES.
THE BREAD PANS ARE EMPTY.
THE OVEN IS STILL.
IT'S TIME FOR A NEW LIFE FOR
    OURSELVES.

THANK YOU FOR YOUR PATRONAGE
THROUGH 3 GENERATIONS OF OUR
FAMILY. WE WILL MISS YOU.

Don + Marcia Dietz

JUNE 2010

"It's all over." The Dietz Bakery closing sign. *Bonnie Hahn Martin.*

The bakery also made cinnamon rolls, coffee cakes and doughnuts. I gain a pound just thinking about them.

But any way you slice it, the bread was the star attraction. Dietz bread was front and center at thousands of family dinners, birthdays, wedding parties and special occasions. There are quite a few locals still around who remember walking home, cradling Dietz bread, the loaf wrapped in white paper, still warm from the oven.

In Fredericksburg, Dietz had a corner on the bread market. When I first came to town, I took a loaf of ordinary store-bought bread to a party. Big mistake. Nobody would touch it. I was the butt of bread jokes for months.

Many of the people I talked to remember the aroma of Dietz Bakery more than anything else. The smell of freshly baked bread overwhelmed the brain and erased all other thoughts from the mind. It lured customers, even tourists, to Dietz's door, drawn by an irresistible force.

Looking back, it's hard for me to separate the bread from the culture and the times that produced it. Dietz Bakery, like the people of Fredericksburg, forged ahead through good times and bad. Dietz supplied this community with bread through World War II, numerous armed conflicts, the Cold War, hippies, the moon landing, Watergate, disco, the fall of the iron curtain and 9/11.

A loaf of Dietz bread was a taste of history and one of those rare things worth standing in line for.

27

IRON BREW

If you remember Iron Brew, you've been around Gillespie County for a while. For everyone else, Iron Brew is not German moonshine cooked up in a rusty copper kettle but a legendary soft drink once bottled by the Kraus family of Fredericksburg.

The origins of Iron Brew are as mysterious as Donald Trump's tax returns or Hillary Clinton's emails. It probably began in the 1880s as a concoction mixed by MacNish & Son, the owners of a sugar plantation near Kingston, Jamaica.

MacNish's Iron Brew was a sweet beverage made by blending pure cola nut with iron and spices. MacNish sold it not as a soft drink but as an elixir, guaranteed to regulate the stomach and nervous system to relieve headaches, nausea and dyspepsia.

Certain doctors who claimed no connection to the company swore by Iron Brew. Their recommended dosage was at least two to three glasses a day—the more the better.

But soon, Jamaicans started drinking the stuff, not for medicinal purposes but because it tasted good. Jamaicans especially liked to drink Iron Brew mixed with fresh cow's milk.

Beginning in 1889, the Maas and Waldstein Chemical Company of New York first marketed a soft drink called Iron Brew in the United States. The connection between MacNish & Son and Mass and Waldstein, if any, is unclear. The New York company may have just taken over the name.

Mass and Waldstein produced the Iron Brew syrup on the East Coast and shipped it all over the United States. Local bottling companies mixed the syrup with other ingredients and bottled the finished product.

The problem was that the Iron Brew syrup was widely copied. There were a lot of imitators out there.

Early advertisements stated that a daily drink of Iron Brew made one "pleasant without intoxication." But those same advertisements cautioned drinkers to be careful, as the imitations tasted so bad, one had to take a swig of the real stuff to kill the unpleasant taste.

In Fredericksburg, Jacob Kraus organized the Kraus Soda Fabrik, later renamed the Fredericksburg Coca-Cola Bottling Company, in 1892. Kraus soon began bottling Iron Brew made from a syrup that sources say came from "back east."

Many Germans in the Hill Country developed a taste for Iron Brew. I've had people tell me its creamy vanilla flavor went well with German sausage and potato soup.

Although Iron Brew was sold from Rhode Island to California, it was not widely distributed. It was sold in isolated pockets, particularly in Texas and the Midwest. A cohesive nationwide distribution network, like the one Coca-Cola would one day create, never developed.

As a result, Iron Brew was often hard to find. The scarcity made people want it more and added to its mystique.

But over time, Iron Brew fell victim to the Coca-Cola juggernaut. As Coke became popular, it squeezed out much of the competition.

A bottle of Iron Brew.
Melanie Kordzik.

By the 1940s, the number of places that bottled and sold Iron Brew dwindled to just a few regional markets. By 1969, Fredericksburg was the only place in Texas, and one of the few places in the entire United States, that still bottled and sold Iron Brew.

Stories about Iron Brew are legendary. You can't make this stuff up.

In 1937, San Marcos attorney Henry C. Kyle and a newspaperman from Lockhart, in search of beer, opened a refrigerator in Medina. There, they found and quickly drank what they believed at the time were the last two bottles of Iron Brew in existence. The story made news all over Texas.

Fredericksburg Bottling Company. *Author's photograph.*

When the Kerrville-based psychedelic rock band the Thirteenth-Floor Elevators went to California in 1966, they took several cases of Fredericksburg's Iron Brew with them. After the band performed on the television show *Where the Action Is*, they gave a six-pack of Iron Brew to host Dick Clark, but Clark wouldn't touch it. He was sure it was spiked with LSD.

The Kraus Family stopped selling Iron Brew in the early 1970s.

Of course, Fredericksburg's Iron Brew is not to be confused with a modern soft drink called Iron Bru—the most popular drink in Scotland, after Scotch.

28

THE FREDERICKSBURG RAILROAD

Fredericksburg waited thirty years for the railroad, but when the train arrived, it was a day late and a dollar short.

In the late nineteenth century, Fredericksburg was an isolated community. It was seventy-five miles of bad roads, steep hills and low water crossings to Austin or San Antonio. It took a week or more for a freight wagon to make a run to San Antonio and back.

What this town needed was a railroad.

In the 1880s, a group of local businessmen, led by Bank of Fredericksburg president Temple D. Smith, began a campaign to build a railroad from a junction near Comfort to Fredericksburg, a distance of twenty-four miles. Other men on the railroad committee included Charles Nimitz, August Cameron, Oscar Krauskopf, L.F. Kneese and Adolph Lucas. A.W. Moursund of Blanco County served as legal counsel.

Because railroads were not cheap, the committee needed investors with deep pockets. A group of Chicago businessmen, including General Grant's son Frederick, was briefly interested in the project, but it never got off the ground.

For twenty-five years the committee considered at least thirty deals from twenty different promoters, but the problem was always the same: engineers believed the hills were too high to ever get the railroad to Fredericksburg.

Then, in 1911, Temple Smith met a former shoe salesman from Kansas City named R.A. Love. Mr. Love dreamed big and talked fast, but he knew how to get things done. He made people believe he could move mountains—or at least tunnel through them. He organized a group of San Antonio investors and made his pitch to the railroad committee. In a few days, the deal was struck.

Months of hard work lay ahead. The main barrier was the "big hill" near the Kendall County line. The hill was a high limestone ridge that separated the Pedernales Valley from the Guadalupe River Watershed.

And there was no way around it or over it. The railroad had to go through it.

For four months, workers chipped and blasted away at both ends of the big hill, and by the end of October, the 903-foot-long tunnel was finished.

On a late October day in 1913, a small crowd gathered near the tracks in Fredericksburg. For more than an hour, adults scanned the hills in the direction of Cain City. Children put their ears to the rails.

Then they heard it—a high lonesome steam whistle accompanied by a cloud of black smoke on the horizon. Several minutes later, the first locomotive rolled into Fredericksburg, covered in grease and soot and spewing vapor like a leaky steam pipe.

That glorious event touched off a massive three-day celebration called the Eisenbahnfest (in English, "the Great Railroad Jubilee"). Temple Smith drove the symbolic last spike. Texas governor Oscar Colquitt made a speech. There was music, food, beer and a parade, although rain washed out the free barbeque dinner that was scheduled for the first day.

What's left of the old Fredericksburg Depot, East Park Street, Fredericksburg. *Author's photograph.*

After the celebration, the Fredericksburg and Northern Railroad got down to business. Six days a week, the train left Fredericksburg at 7:15 a.m., with stops at Cain City, Bankersmith (a new town named after banker Temple Smith) and Mount Alamo before arriving at the junction near Comfort at 9:15 a.m. There, passengers connected with the San Antonio and Aransas Pass train. That train arrived at the San Antonio station at 11:54 a.m. The return train left San Antonio at 2:00 p.m. and arrived in Fredericksburg at 7:50 p.m. Sunday had a different schedule.

But train schedules were exercises in wishful thinking. Delays were common. Rockslides had to be cleared, and herds of cattle and goats had to be removed from the track. Railroad employees sometimes had to chop wood along the way to replenish the coal supply. The soft roadbed caused ties to sink, resulting in derailments. Lacking funds for heavy equipment, passengers and area residents helped right derailed cars. A two-hour trip could take all day.

The delays were nuisances, but a changing economy caused real problems for the new railroad. Highways were improving. Gasoline was cheap. Automobiles gave people the freedom to travel in ways the railroad never could. Trucks were competing successfully with trains for hauling freight.

From the beginning, cash flow problems hounded the railroad, and within a year, the company was in receivership. New investors took over the company and ran it at a loss until 1942, when it was abandoned and sold for scrap.

29

THE TUNNEL

The railroad tunnel through the "big hill" between Fredericksburg and Comfort was an engineering marvel. It was the first—and for a time, the only—railroad tunnel in Texas.

Without the tunnel, the train would never have gotten to Fredericksburg. Steam trains could only climb a 2 percent grade—that's a two-foot rise for every one hundred feet in length.

Engineers sometimes designed switchbacks so trains could climb steep hills and mountains, but a switchback was not possible at the big hill because of right-of-way limitations. They then considered a longer route with easier grades that took the tracks close to Kerrville, but Kerr County residents, who already had a railroad, blocked that route. For Fredericksburg, the tunnel was the only choice.

Workers for the Foster Crane Company began chipping away at the tunnel in April 1913. Ted Carr of Gillespie County supervised the crews that used picks, shovels, scrapers and blasting powder to bore a hole through the limestone hill.

Two crews attacked the hill, one from each side. The crews worked around the clock. Each worker earned fifty cents for an eight-hour shift.

Casual observers and even the railroad workers had doubts that the bores, coming from opposite directions, would actually line up, but the skeptics were wrong. The two crews met in the middle, just as planned, on July 15, 1913.

The tunnel through the Big Hill. *Author's photograph.*

The finished tunnel was a straight bore just over nine hundred feet long—about the length of a football field. It was cut through solid limestone, so it needed no supports.

Once trains began using the tunnel, a daily ritual developed. When the train approached the "big hill," the conductor yelled "tunnel." That was a signal for passengers to close all windows. Otherwise, the coaches would be filled with a thick cloud of coal smoke that belched from the smokestack.

On every trip, north and south, a brakeman walked the length of the tunnel ahead of the locomotive to remove rocks that had been dislodged and fallen since the last run. In the winter, seeping water caused large icicles to form on the ceiling. Those icicles had to be chopped out with an axe before a train could pass.

Animals and varmints of all kinds took refuge in the tunnel. Cattle, sheep and goats congregated there to escape the summer heat and the winter wind. The brakeman who walked ahead of the train carried a pistol to shoot rattlesnakes. In the summer, he might have to reload several times.

Beginning in the 1950s, long after the tunnel was abandoned by the railroad, ranchers were puzzled by what looked like a cloud of smoke swirling up from the tunnel just before nightfall. It wasn't smoke but millions of Mexican free-tailed bats. The cloud was so thick, it confused weathermen. It appeared like a thunderstorm on the radar screen.

The tunnel was an amazing feat of engineering, but it came at a heavy price. The entire cost of the railroad's construction from the junction near Comfort to Fredericksburg, including grading, rights-of-way, rails, ties, terminal grounds and all other costs amounted to $308,500. The cost of the tunnel alone was $134,000, 43 percent of the total. The high cost of the tunnel is one reason the railroad never made a nickel for its investors.

But the bats and the rattlesnakes had no concern for such matters. They moved in when the railroad left and have been there ever since.

30

July Fourth in Fredericksburg

T he thunder of cannon fire at six o'clock in the morning shook plaster from the walls and rattled windows from Kraus Corner to the Nimitz Hotel. When the shooting stopped, the concert band played "Dies ist der Tag des Herrn" (This is the Day of the Lord) before beginning its march down Main Street, pausing at every corner to play a military tune or some John Philip Sousa.

Independence Day has always been celebrated with a little more gusto in Fredericksburg than in a lot of other places. I think it's because the people here understand what the old freedom-loving settlers went through just for the opportunity to build a town on the wild Texas frontier.

These celebrations have always been loud and brassy, and they often included gunfire of some sort. The firing of the cannon at the crack of dawn goes back until at least 1890.

Rubin Bernhard and Harry Land assumed command of the cannon after World War I. They fired the opening salvo from Marketplatz at 5:45 a.m. Then for good measure, in case anyone in a three-mile radius was still in bed, they burned a little more gunpowder from several locations along Main Street.

Young people answered the early morning cannon barrage by shooting anvils. There were dances at Klaerner's Hall (where the Palace Theater is today) and at Klaerner's Park on the Harper Road. The dances started at three o'clock in the afternoon and lasted until daylight the next morning. People didn't get together very often back then, and a lot of traveling was involved, so when they did get together, they made the most of it.

SHERIFF KLAERNER READY TO LEAD PARADE
...with a shotgun accross the saddle

Sheriff Alfred Klaerner leading the parade with a shotgun across his lap. *From the* Fredericksburg Standard.

The 1922 Fourth of July parade included three horseless carriages carrying Civil War veterans. The 1923 celebration featured a baseball game, a rooster catch and a five-mile automobile race. Kelly Field in San Antonio sent a military band and a squadron of airplanes. Radio experts from Fort Sam Houston brought their "powerful receiving apparatus" so sports fans could listen to the Jack Dempsey–Tommy Gibbons heavyweight title bout live from Shelby, Montana. Nobody gave Gibbons a prayer, but the fight went the distance. Dempsey dodged a bullet with a fifteen-round decision. The highlight of the July 4, 1924 celebration was what the *Fredericksburg Standard* billed as a "battle royal," between five or six "rugged individuals" who crawled into the ring in front of the fairground grandstands and wailed on each other until only one was left standing.

The Fourth of July crowd could get a little rowdy. The July 7, 1938 edition of the *Fredericksburg Standard* happily reported that in the course of the most recent celebration, "no one was incarcerated in the county bastille, and the peace officers, with the exception of those who directed traffic, enjoyed as much of a holiday as did the celebrants."

The parade down Main Street, which dates to at least 1891, had grown to be a mile long by 1940. And there was more gunfire. Sheriff Alfred Klaerner rode his roan horse at the front of the parade, occasionally cutting loose with the double-barreled shotgun he carried across his lap.

Calvin Sageser from Harper, known in rodeo circles as the Pecos Kid, rode a wild buffalo at the rodeo held on July 4, 1941. Less than a year later, Sageser joined the marines. On December 15, 1943, Private First-Class Calvin Ode Sageser died while going ashore in New Guinea.

Former president Lyndon Johnson watched the horse races from the grandstands on July 4, 1970. Six days later, Congressman George H.W. Bush, the Republican candidate for U.S. Senate, held a fundraiser in those same grandstands, giving Fredericksburg the distinction of hosting a former president and a future president in less than a week.

If you think about it, modern Independence Day celebrations in Fredericksburg haven't changed all that much. There are still parades, horse races, music, dancing, plenty of food and drink, aircraft flying overhead and thunderous explosions accompanied by the smell of burning gunpowder at the fireworks show.

There's nothing subtle about July 4 in Fredericksburg.

31

FOOTBALL COMES TO FREDERICKSBURG

L ong before it was time for a player to start the game by striking the ball with his toe (the kickoff), the "side liners" (sports fans) had already staked out their territory along the edge of the meadow (the gridiron). The Johnny-come-latelies jostled each other for standing room in the less-desirable area (the cheap seats) behind the scoring region (the endzone).

Yes, the lingo was confusing, but that was understandable, since most people who gathered that day in Fredericksburg had never seen a football game.

Baseball was huge in those days. Most people could name the heavyweight boxing champion. But football in the early twentieth century was an obscure sport played by Ivy Leaguers between the last game of squash and the beginning of lacrosse season.

That all began to change in 1911, when a college freshman from Fredericksburg named Louis Jordan made the football team at the University of Texas. Four years later, journalist Walter Camp listed Jordan on Camp's All-American football squad, making Jordan one of the first players from below the Mason-Dixon line to be named All-American.

Louis Jordan sparked an interest in football in these parts. Friends and relatives of the Jordan family began making the trek to Austin to watch Jordan play. Each year, the caravan got bigger, especially when the Longhorns played the Aggies in Austin on Turkey Day. Slowly, football crept into our collective consciousness.

In August 1920, newspapers carried a story about a bunch of impoverished football fanatics who met in the showroom at Ralph Hay's Hupmobile dealership in Canton, Ohio and founded the National Football League. Even money said the NFL wouldn't last until Christmas, but it outlived the Hupmobile and then some. (Today, an NFL franchise is worth between $2 billion and $7 billion).

A Battlin' Billie football helmet from early 1950s. *Author's photograph.*

That fall, the University Interscholastic League sponsored the first Texas high school football championship. Cleburne and Houston Heights pulverized each other to a scoreless tie.

The military played a key role in popularizing football. After World War I, regimental squads from bases in San Antonio played exhibition football games in surrounding towns. Fredericksburg wanted to host an exhibition game for its Armistice Day celebration in 1921, but the event never happened (Spanish flu was the likely culprit).

Meanwhile, young people all over Gillespie County played informal games on sandlots and school playgrounds. Fredericksburg High School made plans to field a football team as soon as it could scrape up enough money for a ball and some uniforms.

Then, in October 1923, the *Fredericksburg Standard* announced, "Sport lovers of our town have the opportunity of witnessing the first game of football played in the town of Fredericksburg."

On October 21, 1923, a team of young men from Fredericksburg played the Kerrville All-Stars on a field in South Heights, a section of town across Barons Creek, near Columbus Street.

Two weeks later, the *Standard* made another big announcement: "For the first time in the history of our high school, our local high school football team will play against the Kerrville High School football team."

The two rivals battled it out on November 8, 1923, in Fredericksburg on the field in South Heights. For the record, Kerrville won both games, but Fredericksburg was hooked on football.

The whole town got behind the local team. In 1925, Central Drug Company of Fredericksburg bought the guys a new ball. The team treasured that pigskin like Ebenezer Scrooge cherished a farthing.

Each year, the team improved, and on November 27, 1925, Fredericksburg High School played Brady High School for the district championship. The game ended in a tie. Then the news broke that Brady used an ineligible player, so the league declared Fredericksburg district champions.

With help from the Works Progress Administration, the school built a football field with concrete bleachers on College Street. Local businessmen raised money for the lights.

The school dedicated the new lighted field on November 3, 1939, before the Fredericksburg-Lampasas football game. Clyde Littlefield, the legendary University of Texas football and track coach and Longhorn teammate of Louis Jordan, made the dedication speech.

With football now being played on cool evenings during nonworking hours, attendance soared.

It's been soaring ever since.

First Night Football Game in Fredericksburg

On November 3, 1939, Fredericksburg High School and Lampasas High School played a football game. It was not the first time the Hillbillies and Badgers played each other, but this event was historic. It was the first football game played in Fredericksburg under the lights.

Just a few years earlier, the old football field on College Street was not in good shape. There were no bleachers. Bare spots on the playing surface turned into mud holes when it rained. The facility needed an upgrade, but money was tight. The country was in the middle of the Great Depression.

Then, in 1938, the school received a matching grant from the Works Progress Administration in Washington, D.C. With the money the school hired workers to contour the field for better drainage, sod the playing surface with new grass and build a cinder track around the field. The school used the remaining funds to erect a fifty-inch-high fence along College Street and build concrete seating for six hundred.

But it was candlepower that fulfilled the dream of Gillespie County football fans and made the Lampasas game an extraordinary event. With lights, football could be played on cool autumn evenings during nonworking hours. Attendance soared. Although no one saw it coming at the time, lights would transform an unassuming athletic contest into the phenomenon that became Friday night football.

As the big night approached, the whole community pitched in to get the field ready. The class of '39 raised money for new goalposts. The Lion's Club donated a scoreboard. The General Electric Company installed the lights, paid for entirely by local businessmen. Civic leaders organized a pregame dedication ceremony. The guest speaker was Clyde Littlefield, the legendary football and track coach at the University of Texas.

Coach Littlefield was no stranger to Fredericksburg. He played semiprofessional baseball for the Fredericksburg Giants in the early years of the twentieth century, and as a student athlete at the University of Texas, Littlefield was a friend, classmate and teammate of Louis Jordan of Fredericksburg. Jordan played for the Longhorns from 1911 to 1914 and was the first Longhorn football player to be named All-American. But what made Louis Jordan special was his service to his country. Jordan joined the army in 1917 and was commissioned as a lieutenant. He was killed by artillery fire in France, the first officer from Texas to lose his life in World War I.

The dedication of the Fredericksburg Lighted Athletic Stadium was also a reunion of sorts for Coach Littlefield and Fredericksburg High School coach Chester Klaerner. The two men had crossed paths before. The date was October 25, 1930, and they met on a football field in Houston. Littlefield was the head football coach at the University of Texas, and Klaerner played guard for the Rice Owls. That meeting still gave Coach Littlefield heartburn.

The Longhorns, with stars Ernie Koy and Ox Emerson, were heavy favorites going into the game, but Rice came to play. The score was tied 0–0 late in the fourth quarter when Rice punted to Texas. Johnny Craig of the Longhorns fielded the ball on the three yard line, but before he could

The 1935 concrete bleachers at the old football field on College Street, Fredericksburg. *Author's photograph.*

take a step, Chester Klaerner, on punt coverage for the Owls, knocked Craig into the middle of next week. The ball popped loose, and the Owls recovered inside the five yard line. Rice scored on the next play and won the game. It was the only loss for the Longhorns, and it cost them a shot at a national championship.

After Coach Littlefield's dedication speech, it was time to play football. On a cool Friday evening in the Hill Country, a packed house watched the Hillbillies beat the Badgers 27–6.

It doesn't get much better than that.

32

FEMALE ATHLETES
CONFOUND EXPERTS

I f you've ever watched Serena Williams crush a tennis ball or Simone Biles defy gravity, you might be surprised to learn that there was a time when many experts in the fields of athletics and medicine believed women were not as tough as men and were too delicate to play sports. Those experts never met my mother-in-law.

Those beliefs about weak females were strong enough that the University Interscholastic League (UIL), the organization that has governed high school athletics in Texas since the early twentieth century, was slow to accept girls' athletics. (Tennis was an exception.) For sports like basketball, it was up to high school coaches and administrators to get the ball bouncing.

Fredericksburg High School fielded its first girls' basketball team in 1914. There was no organized league then. The girls played any high school team within driving distance.

In the first couple of years, the team could count its wins on one hand with fingers left over. Then, in 1916, the girls beat Kerrville twice and Harper twice. The thrill of victory was contagious.

The girls played close to home those first few years. But the team added Boerne High School to the schedule in 1921 and Blanco in 1924.

Fredericksburg had no gym in those days. The girls played on an outdoor dirt court, weather permitting. If the weather was bad, the team cleared the dance floor at Peter's Hall (on the corner of Main and Orange Streets, where BBVA Compass Bank is today) and played there until the school district built a gym in the early 1930s.

For the first fourteen years the team had no uniforms. "It takes money to buy uniforms," the local newspaper reported in 1928, "and money is hard to get. Perhaps Santa Claus will take pity on good children who are needy and leave at the schoolhouse door, sometime before long, a 'surprise box' for the basketball girls."

Sure enough, on January 12, 1929, a large box arrived at the high school on Travis Street. Inside the box were red and white striped jerseys and red shorts.

Unlike boys, the girls had no opportunity to play for district and state championships in the 1920s and 1930s. Then, in 1938, a group of high school coaches and administrators who believed in girls' athletics formed the High School Girls Basketball League of Texas. Fredericksburg High School joined that group in 1944.

The league assigned member schools to districts. At the end of the year, the district champions met for a state tournament at either Rena Marrs-McLean Gym in Waco or Dowdy Gym in Hillsboro.

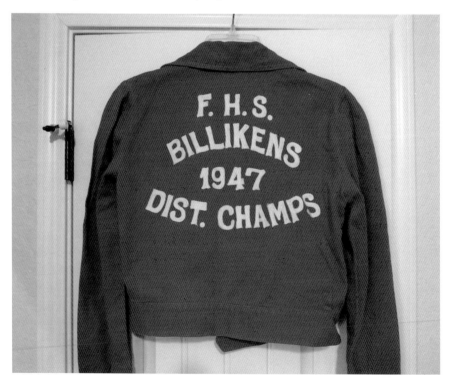

Madeleine Land Oestreich's 1947 district champion jacket. *Author's photograph.*

In 1946, the Fredericksburg High School girls' basketball team didn't lose a game in the regular season and beat San Marcos Academy 30–15 for the district championship. Mabel Henke, a forward, and Madeleine Land, a guard (my mother-in-law), made the All-District team. (Texas girls played six-on-six half-court basketball until the 1970s.)

In March, the team represented Fredericksburg High School in the state tournament in Hillsboro.

With a group of talented underclassmen, the team went back to the state tournament for the next two years. In 1948, the girls won the consolation bracket, beating West Columbia High School 30–22.

That year, the school and the town sent the team on its way in style. There was a big pep rally for the girls broadcast by the local radio station.

The Fredericksburg High School swing band, the Korn Kobblers, accompanied the girls to the state tournament. The band made the trip in Bull Moellering's station wagon.

In those days, the Fredericksburg High School girls' basketball team was called the Billikens. In case you're wondering, a Billiken is a mythical good luck figure that represents "things as they ought to be."

By 1950, girls' basketball was a big success in Fredericksburg and all over Texas. That year the UIL, which had been sponsoring high school boys' football and basketball since 1920, finally agreed to include girls' basketball, as if it had a choice.

Turns out, those experts who said women were too delicate to play sports were wrong. They were probably the same bunch of guys who said women shouldn't vote, preach, run a company or be in politics.

33

ALTER STOLTZ SOLVES
AN IMAGE PROBLEM AT FHS

There is no delicate way to put this. Fredericksburg High School (FHS) once had an image problem. Many people outside Gillespie County mistakenly thought the school's mascot was a hillbilly, not a billy goat. It took a little PR work and a legendary goat named Alter Stolz to clear up the confusion.

In an article published in the *Fredericksburg Standard* some years ago, longtime Fredericksburg head football coach and athletic director Carlin Wicker traced the origins of the FHS mascot controversy to an early twentieth century athletic contest between Fredericksburg High School and Main Avenue High School in San Antonio (later Fox Tech). Although Fredericksburg lost the game, a San Antonio sportswriter wrote, "Those boys from up in the hills [battled Main Avenue] like a bunch of billy goats."

The Fredericksburg athletes, students and fans liked what the sportswriter had written and informally adopted the nickname "Hill Billies" (two words), meaning "billy goats of the hills."

Art Kowert, longtime editor of the *Fredericksburg Standard*, told a similar story. In 1965, he wrote, "No one really knows where the name originated, but it is generally agreed that it started some forty-odd years ago when a *San Antonio Light* sportswriter had trouble getting the name Fredericksburg into a headline and christened the red and white team the Hillbillies."

Bob Klingelhofer, the first FHS football coach, had more information. He told Art Kowert:

In 1924, when it became evident that football was here to stay, it was decided that the team needed a name and a mascot. The high school students submitted a number of names, among them Hillbillies, the billie goat then being and today still is, a valuable [but] cantankerous, hard to handle and smelly member of our Hill Country Society.

And so, on the appointed day, the student body and faculty met in solemn conclave and after carefully considering all names submitted, voted overwhelmingly for the name 'Hillbillies' and designated the billy goat as the official mascot.

A story on page 19 of the 1923–24 *Mesa*, the FHS yearbook, supports Coach Klingelhofer's story.

Wherever the name originated, the people of Fredericksburg always knew the word *hillbilly* referred to a goat. The problem was that the rest of the world didn't get it. Many outsiders thought the FHS mascot was an unsophisticated person from a remote mountainous region. FHS was the butt of quite a few jokes.

FHS head football coach Ewell Sessom helped clarify the issue in the early 1960s, when he began referring to his athletic teams as the "Battlin' Billies," but the rest of the world was slow to catch on. When Carlin Wicker arrived in Fredericksburg in 1963, there was still confusion over whether or not FHS was the Battlin' Billies or the Hillbillies.

The mascot controversy came into focus in 1965, during a bi-district football game with Granbury, when the Granbury pep squad held up a large sign with a drawing of a scruffy backwoodsman that supposedly represented the FHS mascot. The backwoodsman looked like the cartoon character Snuffy Smith.

The sign touched a nerve with Fredericksburg fans. Every time the Granbury pep squad held it up, the Fredericksburg fans, led by former Billie Kermit Rahne, spelled out G-O-A-T-S.

Rahne made it his mission to inform the rest of the world that the FHS mascot was a billy goat. His garage on Main Street came to be called the Goat Shed.

Then Alter Stolz made his historic debut as the FHS mascot at a pep rally on October 21, 1966, prior to the Fredericksburg-Uvalde football game.

The story says that Billie Booster Club member Glenn Quinn came up with the idea of using a live goat as the team mascot. Quinn chose a magnificent angora goat with a spectacular set of horns from Benno Eckert's herd in Willow City. The animal was Benno's bell goat and family pet.

Alter Stolz head in the foyer of Fredericksburg High School. *Author's photograph.*

His name was Alter Stolz. The name means "old pride."

The day of the pep rally, in front of a roaring crowd, Alter Stolz pranced in, nose in the air, looking like he wanted to butt something. He wore a flashy read and white blanket that read "Alter Stolz, FHS, Battlin' Billies." It was a pivotal moment in the history of Fredericksburg High School athletics.

Well, Fredericksburg won the game against Uvalde that night and went on to win the district championship. Whether he deserved it or not, Ol' Alter Stolz got a lion's share of the credit.

Glenn Quinn and Sonny Bonn were the goat's keepers, and they treated Alter Stolz like a king. His majesty got a royal shearing each year at the Pioneer Museum. Dr. Curtis Eckhardt gave him his yearly checkups. And Alter Stolz, never camera shy, always got a wash and a rinse before having his picture taken for the *Mesa.*

Alter Stolz's headstone, Fredericksburg High School. *Author's photograph.*

For several years, Alter Stolz traveled with the football team, and he appeared at many special events. He became a part of the culture. He logged close to seven thousand travel miles in his illustrious career. The publicity he received cleared up the mascot question once and for all.

In 1968, Fredericksburg High School, led by head cheerleader Lizzie Krauskopf (Brookshire), held a schoolwide contest to come up with a motto to go along with the school's new mascot. Student council president Terry Bonn announced the winning motto at the pep rally. "Billie Pride, Uber Alles" became the battle cry that carried the FHS Battlin' Billies to athletic glory.

Alter Stolz died in 1972, but in a way, he's still around. His mounted head is on display at Fredericksburg High School. The rest of him is buried on a hill overlooking the football stadium, where people say his spirit, like a foggy apparition, is sometimes seen hanging over the field, urging the Battlin' Billies on to victory.

Or maybe it's just smoke from the concession stand.

34

NINE PIN BOWLING

Nine pin bowling was once a popular sport in Fredericksburg, but it was an obscure game that never caught on in Texas outside the German communities in the Hill Country. Fifty miles away, few people had even heard of it.

The game of nine pin bowling came to America in the seventeenth century, and for a time, it was a fashionable sport in men's circles. Some men loved it too much, preferring to spend Sundays at the bowling alley instead of church.

Bowling alleys, like pool halls, acquired sleazy reputations. Women and church officials were so unhappy with bowling—not to mention the drinking and gambling associated with the sport—they persuaded several state and local governments to pass laws making nine pin bowling illegal.

To get around the new laws, some genius added a tenth pin, and the rest is history. By the twentieth century, ten pin bowling had far surpassed nine pin bowling in popularity with the public.

Ten pin really took off after World War II when automatic pin setters and electronic scoring made the game faster and easier. At the same time owners of bowling establishments cleaned up their act. Bowling "alleys" became bowling "lanes." Bowling became respectable.

Throughout the evolution of ten pin bowling, the game of nine pin remained stranded in the nineteenth century, untainted by anything modern or progressive. Because there were no automatic pin setters, the pins were set by hand. Players kept score on a chalkboard. The game honored tradition,

Fischer Bowling Club, Fischer. *Author's photograph.*

refused to change and slowly faded from popular culture. By the 1980s, the German Hill Country, where tradition and heritage are treasured, was about the only area in the United States where the game was played. It is still played today in a few isolated pockets northwest of San Antonio.

Nine pin is a noisy, sociable game. It is a team sport, with plenty of time between turns for drinking and fraternizing. The rules are simple. The pins are set in the shape of a diamond. The center pin, called the kingpin or redhead, has a special red mark. A team gets nine points when it knocks down all nine pins but twelve points when it knocks down all pins but the kingpin. There are six people on a team, and each team bowls six frames or innings. Each team is led by a captain who gets to pick the bowling order. He will say his decision is based on a detailed analysis of the situation and intimate knowledge of each bowler's ability, but it usually comes down to who's buying the beer.

The Germans of Fredericksburg and the Hill Country, more than any other group I know, value leisure time and emphasize it in their community life. They play just as hard as they work and feel no guilt about it. A generation ago in Fredericksburg, there were singing societies and shooting groups.

There were dances and concerts. Some families spent every Saturday night enjoying the company of other families at the ice house down the street. But for much of the twentieth century, nine pin bowling consistently drew the largest crowds.

There was a time in Fredericksburg when bowling leagues were active Monday through Saturday at Hermann Sons Hall and at the four lanes at Turner Hall. There were men's leagues, women's leagues and mixed leagues, and there was a waiting list to get in—that's because nine pin bowling, more than anything else, was a social event. Skill level was not important, and even the score was a secondary concern. Nine pin was about laughing and drinking beer. It was about fun. It was about belonging and even romance. I know a surprising number of couples who bowled nine pin on their first date. Quite a few Fredericksburg husbands met their wives at a mixed league night at Turner Hall.

But times change. Outside influences have altered traditional cultural patterns in the Hill Country. Fredericksburg is both a victim and beneficiary of that change. Still, it's too bad no one bowls nine pin in Fredericksburg anymore.

35

LEGENDS AND GIANTS

All the talk about the Houston Astros in the World Series reminds me that baseball has been a part of life in Fredericksburg and Gillespie County since the beginning of the twentieth century.

The Germans who settled the Texas Hill Country took to baseball. By the 1920s, small towns all over Gillespie and the surrounding counties had adult baseball teams. There were once twenty-three different adult baseball teams in Gillespie County alone.

Baseball was the perfect game for the isolated rural communities in the Hill Country. Just about anyone could play. There was no expensive equipment required; teams needed only a bat, a ball and an open space.

In the early days, there was no radio or television in the Hill Country. Baseball was the biggest show in town from April to September. One of the most successful teams in the Hill Country was the Fredericksburg Giants.

A surprising number of Giants went on to play professional baseball at one level or another. Felix Holmig played for the Galveston Sand Crabs in the Texas League. Carl Kott played in the Evangeline League, the Texas League and the Texas-Arizona League. Andy Andrews, who coached at Fredericksburg High School and managed the Giants in the 1930s, was a catcher in the minor leagues. He also became a minor league umpire and then a scout for the Houston Astros, Milwaukee Brewers and Los Angeles Dodgers. Max Molberg, the manager of the Giants in the 1940s, played for Abbeville, Louisiana, in the Evangeline League and for Gainesville, Texas, in the Big State League.

The Klaerner family of Fredericksburg was famous in the world of baseball. Brothers Hugo, Chester and Alphons all played professional baseball, as did cousins Elias and Phillip.

Chester Klaerner turned down a contract with the Cincinnati Reds in 1932 to finish his degree at Rice. He threw two no-hitters as a pitcher in the Southwest Conference. After college, Chester played in the New York Giants organization. In 1935, he won eighteen games for Tyler in the West Dixie League. He came home in 1937 to coach the Battlin' Billie football team.

Hugo Klaerner in his Chicago White Sox uniform. *Travis Klaerner.*

Hugo Klaerner won twenty games for the Longview Cardinals in 1933, including a perfect game. The big righthander won twenty-four games for Pine Bluff in the East Dixie League before being called up to the majors. In 1934, he appeared in three games with the White Sox and then spent thirty years as the Gillespie County sheriff.

In the early days, the Giants played at the old fairgrounds. There was no outfield fence. A batter had to hit one to the horse track to have time to make it all the way to home plate.

Fans of the Fredericksburg Giants got to see legends play the game. Clyde Littlefield, the renowned football and track coach of the University of Texas, played for the Giants in the early twentieth century.

One afternoon in the 1920s, the San Antonio Public Service team came to Fredericksburg for a game with the Giants. The San Antonio pitcher was Van Bibber, a young army recruit stationed at Fort Sam Houston in San Antonio. Van Bibber, a flame-throwing Arkansas righthander was really Private Jerome "Dizzy" Dean.

The Detroit Tigers once played an exhibition game against the San Antonio Bears at the old fairgrounds field. Detroit Hall of Famer Harry "Slug" Heilmann thrilled the crowd when he hit a ball that landed in the middle of the racetrack.

Dizzy Dean's brother, Paul "Daffy" Dean, played there with a minor league team from Borger.

In the 1940s, Coach Billy Disch could often be seen in the stands, scouting prospects for his Longhorn baseball team.

Hall of Famer Harmon Killebrew played at the old fairgrounds field with a barnstorming group before he made it to the big leagues.

A prominent local business now occupies the site of the old fairgrounds field, where legends and Giants once played the great America game. Something to think about when you're pushing your shopping cart across the crowded parking lot at the Fredericksburg HEB.

36

J.L. YARBOROUGH

A Passion for Baseball

J.L. Yarborough made a lot of money selling coffee for the Nueces Coffee Company of Corpus Christi, but he always seemed to be selling coffee wherever there was a baseball game.

Born in 1893, J.L. Yarborough opened a cleaning business in Hamlin in 1913. In 1914, he married Ruth Owen and moved to Fredericksburg.

Yarborough owned one of the first cleaning and pressing businesses in the Hill Country. His store was located next to Kolmeier and Klier on Main Street.

A business opportunity brought Yarborough to Fredericksburg. As a bonus, he got to play right field for the Fredericksburg Giants baseball team.

You see, J.L. Yarborough had a gift for business, but baseball was his passion.

In 1919, Yarborough sold his cleaning store to Max and Felix Stehling. He moved to San Antonio, where he became a stockholder in the San Antonio Bears of the Texas League. He served as the secretary of the club and later as vice-president.

In 1927, J.L. Yarborough and his brothers founded the Nueces Coffee Company in Corpus Christi. As Yarborough made sales calls, he beat the bushes for baseball talent.

Yarborough could spot a baseball player in a crowded theater. The *San Antonio Light* called him "Old Sleuth." He was "a born baseball scout. He may sell coffee, but he talks, thinks, eats and sleeps baseball."

In 1928, Yarborough saw Joe Moore playing baseball in Crystal City and signed Moore to a Texas League Contract. Moore played in San Antonio for one year before moving to the big leagues.

For twelve seasons, Joe Moore was an intimidating left-handed leadoff hitter for the New York Giants. He was a six-time All- Star. Moore always said he would make Yarborough a guest if the Giants ever played in the World Series.

On an October morning in 1933, Yarborough received a telegram asking him how many tickets to the World Series he wanted. The Giants would be playing Washington in the Fall Classic. Joe Moore invited Yarborough to "come to the series at my expense."

Four days later, Yarborough, his wife and their young son left San Antonio for the East Coast. They watched the Giants beat Carl Hubbell and the Senators in five games.

In addition to Joe Moore, J.L. Yarborough signed or recommended infielder Fats Hetherly from Lampasas (Detroit Tigers), pitcher Joe Vance from Devine (Chicago White Sox and New York Yankees) and pitcher Hugo Klaerner from Fredericksburg (Chicago White Sox).

In the 1930s, Yarborough invented point ball, a form of baseball played by six players. Like six-man football, point ball was meant to be played in small rural communities that didn't always have nine players to field a baseball team.

A point ball field is a triangle instead of a diamond. There are three bases, each ninety feet apart. Each team has two infielders, two outfielders, a pitcher and a catcher. The ball is slightly larger and lighter than a regulation baseball, and the bat is shorter.

In point ball, the batter is out after a second strike. Three balls constitute a walk.

Yarborough staged exhibition games all over Texas, including in the Hill Country. He hoped the game would catch on, but baseball fans missed the point.

As a publicity gimmick, J.L. Yarborough staged the All Brothers Baseball Championship Game between the nine Deike brothers' team from Hye, Texas, and the nine Stanczak brothers' team from Waukegan, Illinois. According to the *Fredericksburg Standard*, J.L. Yarborough "was instrumental in getting the Deike boys interested in playing in the family tournament." Yarborough arranged for the Nueces Coffee Company to buy uniforms for the Deike brothers and to pay their expenses to the game in Wichita, Kansas.

The All Brothers Championship Baseball Game of 1935, won by the Stanczaks, is part of baseball legend. Carlton Stowers told the story in his book *Oh Brother How They Played the Game.*

In the 1940s, J.L. Yarborough and his wife retired to a ranch near Comfort, but he continued to make business calls in South Texas for the Nueces Coffee Company.

It was a good excuse to watch a baseball game.

37

LBJ AND THE POLITICS
OF BARBECUE

There's something about a Texas barbecue that puts people at ease and in the mood to talk turkey. No one understood that phenomenon better than President Lyndon Johnson.

LBJ was a master politician, skilled in the art of persuasion, and no one was better at using, food, drink and ambiance to bend strong-willed men his way.

Johnson first showed a flair for barbecue diplomacy in 1959, when, as senate majority leader and presidential candidate, he hosted a cowboy-style cookout for Mexican president Adolfo Lopez-Mateos at the LBJ Ranch near Stonewall. Guests included Speaker Sam Rayburn and former president Harry Truman.

Then, in 1961, Vice President Johnson planned an even bigger Texas barbecue to honor West German chancellor Konrad Adenauer. Some East Coast Ivy Leaguers in the Kennedy administration scoffed at the idea, but LBJ had the last laugh.

The ranch, with its wide-open spaces and atmosphere of informality, turned out to be an excellent place for heads of state to do business. Foreign dignitaries who usually suffered the stiff formalities of Washington, D.C., or New York now experienced the myth and legend of the American West. They rode horses and watched cattle graze along the lazy Pedernales River.

The ranch had a romantic appeal to Europeans and when combined with the vice president's formidable personality gave LBJ a significant home court advantage when it came to negotiating.

LBJ's ranch gatehouse, Stonewall. *Author's photograph.*

Even the Hill Country's setting played into the hands of the host. German immigrants settled this part of the Texas in the 1840s, and the area had a European flavor in its culture, attitudes, folkways and language. Adenauer could not help but feel that he was among his own kind.

Over the next two years, the vice president invited numerous world leaders and celebrities to the ranch to experience cowboy cuisine. Guests included Field Marshall Mohammed Ayub Kahn of Pakistan and the seven Mercury astronauts.

These events worked so well that Johnson planned his biggest bash yet for November 23, 1963, to coincide with President Kennedy's trip to the Lone Star State, but that barbecue never happened. An assassin killed the president in Dallas and threw America into a tailspin.

Then, barely a month into his presidency, Lyndon Johnson laid plans for the first presidential barbecue in history to honor the new West German chancellor Ludwig Erhard. President Johnson had big problems to solve—the Soviet threat and the Berlin Wall—and he needed the chancellor to see things his way.

Bring on the barbecue.

Famed Fort Worth pit master Walter Jetton catered the rustic repast on Sunday, December 29, 1963. Originally, the meal for three hundred was to be served under the live oak trees in front of the ranch house on the banks of the Pedernales River, but a chilly weather report (the temperature that morning was twenty-seven degrees) moved the event to the gymnasium at the public school in Stonewall, just across the river.

The president's staff brought in hay bales, wagon wheels, saddles, rolls of barbed wire and cedar posts to give the gym an outdoorsy feel. A mariachi band played as the guests arrived.

Walter Jetton served ribs, brisket, ranch-style beans, German potato salad, sourdough biscuits and Texas coleslaw from the back of a chuck wagon. There were fried fruit pies for dessert, along with Jetton's famed "six-shooter coffee—so strong it will float a .44," and lots of beer.

In addition to Chancellor Erhard was a passel of dignitaries, including Secretary of State Dean Rusk, presidential press secretary Pierre Salinger, West German foreign minister Gerhard Schroder, Senator Ralph Yarborough, director of the Marshall Space Flight Center in Alabama Werner von Braun, Secret Serviceman Rufus Youngblood and Miss Texas 1963 Linda Loftis.

Humorist and Austin TV personality Cactus Pryor was the emcee for the event, and he added just the right touch of comedy and reverence in light of recent tragic events.

The entertainment for the day was an eclectic mix of song and dance. A folk trio called the Wanderers Three sang "This Land Is Your Land," a chorale from St. Mary's Catholic School in Fredericksburg sang "Deep in the Heart of Texas" in German and the Fredericksburg High School Billiettes performed a traditional Bavarian song and dance routine. Van Cliburn added a touch of sophistication to the proceedings when he played Beethoven's Op. 57, known as the "Appassionata," on a baby grand piano next to a stack of hay bales.

After the music, President Johnson presented Chancellor Erhard and his entire delegation with gray Stetson hats in the same "open road" style worn by the president. Chancellor Erhard, looking relaxed and content, donned his Stetson and puffed on a stogie to the delight of the crowd.

No one knows if the great sparerib summit in Stonewall achieved all the outcomes President Johnson intended, but chances are that it did. And even if it fell short, everyone agreed that the first-ever presidential barbecue was a state dinner for the record books.

38

The Johnson Treatment

O n December 21, 1966, a group of Democratic governors met with
Lyndon Johnson at the LBJ Ranch in Stonewall. The governors
were concerned with the volume of the president's Great Society
programs and were certain they could persuade him to take a different
course of action.

The Texans at the Alamo had a better chance.

Say what you will about Lyndon Johnson, he was a formidable political
force. As senate majority leader, no one was better at operating the machinery
of government, and he had few equals in the art of persuasion.

Johnson could twist arms with the best of them. A rival once claimed he
could "sell sand to an Arab."

LBJ got results, but his methods were not easy to pin down. He didn't
have a typical politician's personality or demeanor. He wasn't smooth, good
looking, highly intelligent or particularly likeable. He was an enigma, even
to politicians in Washington.

Senator Richard Russell of Georgia noted, "He doesn't have the best
mind on the Democratic side of the Senate. He isn't the best orator. He
isn't the best parliamentarian. But he's got the best combination of all
these qualities."

Johnson's method of persuasion was a complex combination of techniques
often described as "the Johnson Treatment."

His ability to persuade began with his physical presence. At almost six
feet, four inches tall, Johnson towered over his colleagues. When talking

politics, he loomed over and leaned into the other person. He intimidated people with his size and proximity.

He was a big man with an explosive temper. People who felt his wrath usually tried to avoid it in the future.

Few politicians had the courage to say no to Lyndon Johnson. Journalists Rowland Evans and Robert Novak wrote that the "tornadic force of his personality when mixed with the oxygen of politics" was usually enough to steamroll most opposition.

In describing the Johnson Treatment, Evans and Novak noted, "Its tone could be supplication, accusation, cajolery, exuberance, scorn, tears, complaint and hint of threat. It was all of these together. It ran the gamut of human emotions. Its velocity was breathtaking and all in one direction."

The Johnson Treatment was relentless. It wore people down. It could last a few minutes or several hours, however long it took to get the job done.

The Johnson Treatment was in full force at the December 1966 closed-door meeting with the governors at the LBJ Ranch.

Six days prior to that meeting, the group of unhappy Democratic governors met in White Sulphur Springs, West Virginia. The governors complained that the president was pushing his Great Society programs along too far and too fast. They accused the president of acting unilaterally. They wanted better communication between the White House and the state capitals.

The governors claimed that the Great Society was becoming a political liability and was hurting them in the polls. They argued that the recent swing in favor of the Republicans was a protest against the president and his policies.

One angry governor told the press that unless the president mended his ways, he would be a liability as the head of the Democratic ticket in 1968. The group demanded a meeting with the president, who was on a working vacation at the LBJ Ranch in Stonewall.

The president heard news reports from the meeting in West Virginia and was unhappy that the Democratic governors had gone rogue and were not toeing the party line.

"Come on down to the *Purr*denales," the president said. "We'll talk."

There are no official records of that meeting, although it would have been fun to be a fly on the wall. What we do know is that after the full-blown Johnson Treatment, Iowa governor Harold Hughes, the chairman and spokesman for the governors, came outside to meet with members of the press under the oak trees in front of the Texas White House. With little emotion, he read the following statement before boarding the plane back to Des Moines: "We leave here in complete support of the policies, the principles and the precepts as set forth by the president of the United States....No further comment."

39

STONEWALL BARBECUE
HONORS LBJ

In the Texas Hill Country, nothing says "party" like sweet-smelling, eye-burning barbecue smoke, and judging by the size of the cloud that hung like a fog bank over U.S. Highway 290, the party at the Stonewall Rodeo Arena must have been a whopper.

Most of the time, the traffic rolled through this tiny hamlet between Johnson City and Fredericksburg without stopping or even slowing down, but August 29, 1964, was no typical Saturday night.

The president of the United States was back in town.

Let's just say it had been a big week for President Lyndon Johnson. Two days earlier, he celebrated his fifty-sixth birthday.

To make the occasion even sweeter, that very week, at the Democratic National Convention in Atlantic City, New Jersey, the Democrats chose LBJ as their presidential candidate. His name was the only one placed in nomination. The convention dispensed with the usual theatrics of a roll call vote and nominated him by acclamation.

LBJ was at the pinnacle of his political power. Never again would his popularity or influence be so great.

People in Paris and London imitated his drawl. His mug was famous all over the world—right up there with Elvis and the Beatles.

On Saturday, August 29, the president and Lady Bird were back in Texas after a hectic week in New Jersey. Senator Hubert Humphrey from Minnesota, the Democratic vice-presidential nominee, and his wife, Muriel, traveled to Stonewall with the Johnsons for some quiet rest and relaxation at the LBJ Ranch.

But Stonewall and the Gillespie County Democrats had something else in mind. They fired up the barbecue pit and threw a traffic-stopper of a party for the president at the Stonewall Rodeo Arena.

The Democratic chairmen from a fourteen-county area sold tickets to the event for $2.50. Organizers expected a crowd of 3,000, but 4,600 showed up.

Volunteers hauled wood for three days to cook two tons of beef. Emil Birck of Birck's Bar-B-Que in Fredericksburg was the pit boss.

The party began at 5:00 p.m., but the president and his entourage did not arrive until 8:00. By then, the crowd had already feasted on barbecue, ranch-style beans, potatoes and homemade bread.

Suddenly, a line of black limos pulled up next to the arena. The crowd broke into a cheer when President Johnson stepped into the spotlight.

Right on cue, the Fredericksburg High School Band played a stirring rendition of "Hello Lyndon," the President's official campaign song.

LBJ statue, Stonewall. *Author's photograph.*

"Hello Lyndon" sounded exactly like "Hello Dolly," the hit song from the Broadway musical of the same name.

The program began as soon as the dignitaries found their folding chairs. Harold Carr from radio station KNAF in Fredericksburg was the master of ceremonies. The St. Mary's High School Marychorale performed "The Song of Fredericksburg," written by Fredericksburg native Sister Elaine of Our Lady of the Lake College in San Antonio. The Fredericksburg High School Billiettes kicked up some dust with a dance routine.

By the time Cactus Pryor of KTBC Television in Austin stepped to the microphone, the crowd was ready for some political nonsense. Pryor introduced the Geezinslaws, a musical/comedy act from Austin, who performed a new song called "The Ballad of Barry Goldwater." The song, sung to the tune of "Cool Water," by the Sons of the Pioneers, was a musical jab at Johnson's Republican opponent in the upcoming presidential election.

President Johnson sent word that he would not speak at the event, but when he got there, he changed his mind. He spoke for twenty-five minutes.

After the president spoke, an enormous birthday card unfurled from above. Then organizers hauled in two giant birthday cakes. One cake was made in the shape of the Unites States. The other cake spelled out LBJ.

Someone handed President Johnson a knife and asked him to cut the cake shaped like the United States. With great delight, he plunged the knife straight into the heart of Arizona, the home state of his Republican rival, Barry Goldwater.

The president shook a few thousand hands that evening. The crowd slowly drifted away. By midnight, the party at the Stonewall Rodeo Arena was over.

The smell of barbecue hung around for days.

40

Deer Hunting with JFK and LBJ

I t seemed only natural that a visit to Gillespie County by the guy who was about to become the most powerful man in the free world coincided with the opening of deer season, although I do have trouble seeing John Fitzgerald Kennedy of Massachusetts sitting in a Hill Country deer blind, dressed in camo and soaked in Buck Bomb.

Kennedy was young, handsome, charismatic, Harvard-educated and a member of one of America's wealthiest East Coast families. He was friends with Frank Sinatra, Bing Crosby and Dean Martin. Peter Lawford was his brother-in-law. There were rumors that he had Marilyn Monroe's phone number in his rolodex.

I always believed JFK's idea of an outdoor sport was drinking Dom Perignon on his yacht off Hyannis Port.

In November 1960, Kennedy had just been elected president of the United States. He and his running mate, Lyndon Johnson, beat Republicans Richard Nixon and Henry Cabot Lodge in a close election on November 8.

John Kennedy was a political rockstar to much of the world, but Gillespie County wasn't impressed. The county voted Republican down the line. Even Lyndon Johnson couldn't swing the county for the Democrats. Stonewall was the only Gillespie County precinct to vote for Kennedy-Johnson—the first time in history Stonewall supported the Democratic ticket.

Kennedy was on his way to go slumming in West Palm Beach when he accepted an invitation from Lyndon and Lady Bird to make an overnight stop in Stonewall. Jackie Kennedy was in Washington, nine months pregnant with John Kennedy Jr. JFK may have agreed to the visit to try and dispel

Washington gossip that LBJ and the Kennedys got along like the Suttons and Taylors.

The plane carrying the president-elect arrived at Bergstrom AFB in Austin at 5:55 p.m. on Wednesday, November 16, 1960. LBJ, Lady Bird, Texas governor Price Daniel and Senator Ralph Yarborough met the plane. It was the first face-to-face meeting between Kennedy and Johnson since the election.

At Bergstrom, the group boarded a Lockheed Lodestar for the short flight to the LBJ Ranch in Stonewall. A large group of reporters, including Art Kowert of the *Fredericksburg Standard*, was at the ranch when the plane landed. Norman J. Deitel of the *Fredericksburg Radio-Post* was scheduled to be there but "was unable to get away that afternoon, as our paper had not gone to press, and we were unable to complete our paper until that evening."

Secret Servicemen and ranch security held the press behind barriers until the plane landed. Then things got a little crazy. Art Kowert, unaccustomed to the frenzy of the national press corps, wrote that "newsmen went on a worse stampede than any herd of cattle we've ever seen."

Lyndon and Lady Bird immediately escorted Kennedy to a nearby hangar, where a group of Johnson's neighbors from Stonewall and Blanco County waited. Simon Burg presented Kennedy with a Stetson 100 hat, size seven and a half, and a leather carrying case.

It was like someone handed Kennedy an invitation to Fidel Castro's birthday party. An *Austin American-Statesman* reporter wrote that JFK "held the hat like it had a bomb in it."

Some members of the press urged the president-elect to put it on, but Kennedy, not wanting his hair mussed, refused.

By that time, it was dark, but Johnson insisted on the group taking a road trip along the Pedernales River. LBJ showed Kennedy the Johnson family's cemetery, the house where he was born and the schoolhouse where he first attended classes.

That evening, Governor Daniel, Senator Yarborough and Lieutenant Governor Ben Ramsey joined Kennedy and the Johnsons for dinner at the LBJ Ranch. Speaker of the House Sam Rayburn was supposed to be there, but stormy weather over the Hill Country prevented him from flying in.

Bright and early the next morning, Johnson took Kennedy on the president-elect's first deer hunt. Kennedy killed two bucks: a six-pointer and an eight-pointer. LBJ also killed two bucks, but the number of points was not reported.

I guess deer hunting is like golf. If you shoot a better score than the boss, you better not brag about it.

41

LYNDON'S LITTLE BROTHER

eing a lifelong little brother myself, I understand that big brothers and little brothers have a complicated relationship. Little brothers can be a pain to big brothers, especially if little brother is a free spirit and big brother is someone important—like the president of the United States.

One of the more famous presidential little brothers was Billy Carter. While his older brother Jimmy was politicking for the White House, Billy almost ran the family peanut business into the ground.

Billy wasn't much of a businessman, but he was a wiz at drinking beer, telling dirty jokes and taking money from the Libyans.

But Billy Carter wasn't the first presidential little brother to take a walk on the wild side. Before Billy Carter, there was Sam Houston Johnson. Remember him?

Sam Johnson, Lyndon Johnson's little brother, was just as colorful and entertaining as Billy Carter—it's just that Sam's brother was better than Billy's brother at keeping scandalous stories out of the *Washington Post* and the *New York Times*. I think I read somewhere about a full-time White House staffer whose job was to keep Sam from causing presidential embarrassment.

Still, Sam was always good for a fill on a slow news day, usually to the humiliation of his brother, the president.

Sam was earthy and outspoken. He gambled, hung out with questionable characters, passed a few bad checks and stretched the truth from here to San Antone.

But it was drinking that got Sam into trouble over and over again. He drank "to make other people look interesting."

One night in Brownsville, Texas, Sam hit the sauce a little too hard and got thrown in jail. The White House staffer in charge of embarrassment prevention asked local authorities to quietly release the first brother, but Sam, in true little brother fashion, said he was just fine where he was and stayed until morning.

Despite living in LJB's shadow, Sam said he wouldn't trade places with his brother for all the tea in China. Sam even claimed Lyndon secretly envied his younger brother's carefree lifestyle and that LBJ's anger at Sam's drinking, gambling and carousing was partly caused by jealousy.

Sam had a law degree but never went near a courtroom, except as a defendant. He spent his life in government jobs as an advisor to his brother.

Of course, working for LBJ would drive anyone to drink—or, as Sam put it, "Anyone who works for Lyndon more than thirty days ought to receive a Purple Heart."

In 1970, Sam wrote a book called *My Brother Lyndon*. LBJ thought the book was a little too candid and punished Sam the way he punished anyone who displeased him—he gave Sam a good dose of the silent treatment.

Historian Robert Caro, while doing research on his famous work on LBJ, *The Path to Power*, interviewed Sam, but "the interviews were very unproductive, or to be more exact, they were very unreliable. In the first place, Sam Houston Johnson drank a lot. He also talked with a bravado that made you rather distrustful of what he said. And when I would try to check out the various stories he told me, too often, they weren't true."

Several years later, Caro met Sam on the street in Johnson City and found Sam a changed man. He had stopped drinking and started going to church.

On the eve of Jimmy Carter's inauguration, Sam Johnson had some free advice for first brother–elect Billy Carter: "Don't drink at the White House. Don't say anything on the White House telephone unless you want the whole damn world to know about it. Don't advise the president unless you know what you are talking about. It could be dangerous for the country."

Sam Houston Johnson filed for bankruptcy in 1973. He spent his last years in a room at the Alamo Hotel in Austin and a small house in Johnson City. He died in 1978 and was buried at the Johnson family cemetery in Stonewall.

Being a little brother is sometimes a blessing and sometimes a curse.

"I was Lyndon's brother," Sam used to say. "You can't get any higher than that—or any lower."

42

BROCCOLI SIGN HALTS
BUSH MOTORCADE

When President George H.W. and Barbara Bush came to Fredericksburg on March 3, 1993, we were told not to get too excited about it. We would see them in passing—for a few seconds at most and from the neck up—in the backseat of a limo.

Getting up close and personal with the former president and first lady was out of the question—no exceptions.

Security was as tight as a Yeti cooler, except for one detail: the Secret Service forgot to brief Ms. Parker's class.

Some of you may remember that visit was right after Bush 41 made all those comments about a certain green stalky vegetable.

It began at a Florida fundraiser with a bad joke: "I've made it very clear how I feel about raising taxes," the president said. He paused for dramatic effect. "I'd rather have broccoli for breakfast."

At the time, America was in a fitness phase, and not everyone was happy about it. Us pizza and doughnut guys were looking frantically for relief from the kale and carrot juice crowd.

Whether you agreed with his politics or not, George H.W. Bush was a regular guy. Like many of us, he preferred a hot dog and a beer to a cauliflower and goat cheese sandwich with a soy milk chaser. And this president's opinion had clout. When President Bush expressed a preference for pork rinds, sales of that great southern delicacy jumped 11 percent.

George H.W. Bush was not one to dodge an unpleasant subject. When he was pressed about the broccoli business, he gave it to us stalk and all.

"I do not like broccoli," he confessed, "and I haven't liked it since I was a little kid and my mother made me eat it. Well, I'm president of the United States, and I'm not going to eat any more broccoli."

"By golly, I'm the president," he said, raising his fist in the air. "No more broccoli."

There was a breaking news flash on CNN. The chairman of the Republican National Committee threw up his hands. "There goes the broccoli vote."

Bush immediately issued an executive order outlawing broccoli at the White House and on board Air Force One. The Democrats questioned the legality of the order, saying it was "in the twilight zone of dubious constitutional legitimacy."

Congressional Republicans seized the moment. "The president feels about taxes the same way he feels about broccoli," said an Arizona congressman when arguing against a tax bill. "You can put it on the table in front of him, but he's not going to eat it."

Then Bill Clinton beat George H.W. Bush in the 1992 presidential election. Experts are still analyzing the role of broccoli in that contest. They've written several thick books about it.

George and Barbara Bush, out of office for just five weeks, came to Fredericksburg in March 1993 for a private view of the Gallery of the

Mrs. Parker's class's broccoli sign, Main Street, Fredericksburg. *Author's photograph.*

President Bush and the broccoli sign, Main Street, Fredericksburg. *Author's photograph.*

Pacific War at the Nimitz Museum. Plans were already underway to name the gallery after President Bush, who was a navy pilot in World War II.

The Bushes' jet landed at Louis Schreiner Field in Kerrville at 9:20 that morning. At 10:00 a.m., their motorcade left for Fredericksburg.

As I remember, it was a cloudy day. A line of identical black cars rolled into town on the Kerrville Highway and slowly turned right on Main Street. All eyes strained to see which car George H.W. and Barbara Bush were in.

Suddenly, there they were, waving to the people on both sides of the street.

Then something in the crowd caught Barbara's eye. George saw it, too. It was a sign made by elementary school students that read, "Out With Broccoli—In With Sauerkraut."

George told the driver to stop. Then George and Barbara got out of the car to mingle with the sign makers in Ms. Parker's class.

The Secret Service scrambled. Those guys don't like surprises. The rest of us had the thrill of a lifetime.

Words are powerful, just ask George H.W. Bush. He once made a bad joke about a vegetable.

Broccoli has stalked him ever since.

43

A Valentine's Day Gift
from Arthur Godfrey

When Arthur Godfrey landed his plane at the Gillespie County Airport near Fredericksburg on October 15, 1955, he was one of best known entertainers in America. Godfrey, a red-headed, freckle-faced ukulele player, made his name in radio and transitioned easily to television. In 1955, he hosted a daily radio show and two weekly TV shows on CBS in New York. His programs were a medley of music, goofy extemporaneous commercials and uninhibited banter.

Godfrey was a powerful force in the entertainment business. His top-rated TV show *Talent Scouts*, an early-day *America's Got Talent*, gave a shot in the arm to struggling performers Tony Bennett, Pat Boone, Patsy Cline and Roy Clark, but the show's screening staff rejected Elvis Presley and Buddy Holly. The King and the Cricket succeeded anyway.

Godfrey was an experienced pilot. He got his pilot's license in 1929. The plane he flew, a decked-out DC-3, was a gift from his friend Eddie Rickenbacker, a World War I flying ace and the president of Eastern Air Lines. Godfrey regularly flew the plane from his farm in Leesburg, Virginia, to work in New York City.

The old redhead had a controlling personality and famous temper. He was known for buzzing the tower at airports that did not give him the runway he wanted, but he didn't have that problem in Gillespie County. There was no tower and only one runway.

Godfrey had flown from Virginia to the Texas Hill Country that October to visit his old friend Senator Lyndon Johnson, who was laid up at the LBJ Ranch in Stonewall, recuperating from a heart attack.

The *Washington Post* reported that Godfrey made an earlier trip to the LBJ Ranch at the request of his friend, controversial air force general Curtis LeMay. Godfrey, an outspoken proponent of aviation, went down to Stonewall to see "Lyndon" to lobby the senator for his support of the B-52 bomber, one of General LeMay's pet projects.

After landing at the Gillespie County Airport in October 1955, Godfrey spent the night at the LBJ Ranch and then returned to the airport the next day. By the time he arrived, it was late afternoon, and darkness was falling.

As Godfrey prepared to take off, he asked an attendant if the airport had landing lights. When told the airport had no lights, Godfrey responded, "I'll send you some."

On Valentine's Day 1956, several large crates arrived at the Gillespie County Airport, sent in care of Senator Lyndon B. Johnson from Arthur Godfrey in Leesburg, Virginia. The crates held a complete set of landing lights.

After electricians installed the lights, county officials gathered at the airport to throw the switch. Senator Johnson was on hand for the ceremony.

In addition to being an entertainer and a pilot, Arthur Godfrey was a conservationist and a student of ecology. He spoke to groups all over the Unites States about the deterioration of the environment. He wrote three books on the subject.

His interest in the environment and his long friendship with President Johnson and Lady Bird brought him back to Gillespie County in October 1972. He flew in from Virginia as the guest of honor at Mrs. Johnson's Highway Beautification Award ceremony at LBJ State Park.

After the ceremony and the obligatory Hill Country barbecue at the LBJ Ranch, Godfrey and the president talked about Godfrey's visit to the Hill Country seventeen years earlier. Godfrey was pleased to learn that his gift to the Gillespie County Airport was still in use. The two men even talked about the night Godfrey's lights probably prevented a tragedy.

Not long after Gillespie County installed the lights back in 1956, a student pilot who was training at a San Antonio airfield got lost in the dark, spotted the lights and made a safe landing. There is a good chance the pilot would have crashed if the lights had not been installed. The story made news nationwide after Godfrey told it to his radio audience on the air.

Senator Johnson placed the story of Arthur Godfrey's lights and the emergency landing at Gillespie County Airport in the congressional record.

44

BOB HOPE COMES TO FREDERICKSBURG

W hen the directors of the Admiral Nimitz Center in Fredericksburg needed to raise money to restore the old Nimitz Hotel, the occasion called for something bigger than a bake sale or a car wash. So, the directors hot-dialed Hollywood, and Bob Hope answered. On Saturday August 14, 1976, Hope staged the "Stars over the Hill Country" benefit show at the Gillespie County Fairgrounds.

Cousin Minnie Pearl, a star of the *Grand Ole Opry*, made her way from Grinder's Switch, Tennessee, to Fredericksburg to share the stage with Hope. Both entertainers had Fredericksburg connections. Hope was friends with Admiral Nimitz and President Johnson. Minnie Pearl, whose real name was Ophelia Colley, rekindled her acquaintance with Victoria Keidel, Mrs. J. Hardin Perry. They both attended school at Ward-Belmont College, a fashionable girls' school in Nashville.

The big day in Fredericksburg began at 10:30 a.m. with a parade down Main Street from Kraus Corner to the Nimitz Hotel. Minnie Pearl was the grand marshal. A flyover by T-38 jets from Randolph Field in San Antonio scared all the chickens in town.

The new fairgrounds opened that afternoon for an arts and crafts show, and there was music on the stage in front of the grandstands. The acts included Johnny Bush and the Bandoleros, George Chambers and his Country Gentlemen, Darrell McCall, Stoney Edward, Kathy Grissom, Gary Langston—the Singing Sergeant, Inalani and her Hawaiian Dancers, Felix

Pehl's Oompah Band, the singing Feller Family from Harper, the Poverty Playboys, the Wagon Aces and a singer named Jim Owen who sang just like Hank Williams. He looked like him, too.

There was a rumor that the Luckenbach Junior High Band, under the misdirection of the maestro Hondo Crouch, would make a rare public appearance. For weeks prior to the big event, the band gathered in the saloon behind the Luckenbach Store and Post Office, even playing their instruments every once in a while.

Bob Hope's plane landed at the LBJ Ranch at five o'clock that afternoon. He visited the grave of President Johnson and then came directly to the Nimitz for a press conference.

Fredericksburg and the Admiral Nimitz Center pulled out all the stops for the Hollywood legend. Hope, who could not imagine a greater honor than the Congressional Gold Medal President Kennedy gave him in 1963, received a certificate that made him an admiral in the Texas Navy. He then bashed a wall at the hotel with a sledgehammer to symbolize the beginning of its restoration work.

Despite the looming presidential election, Hope smartly avoided politics. "I knew Ronald Reagan since he was a lifeguard," he said when asked if he had a preference, "and I think I played football against Gerald Ford."

Out at the fairgrounds, Max Gardner of San Antonio radio station KKYX was the master of ceremonies for the afternoon entertainment, and Bruce Hathaway, the morning DJ at KTSA, stayed up past his bedtime to emcee the evening show.

Late in the afternoon, the Fredericksburg High School Band entertained the crowd. Then at 7:30 p.m., Minnie Pearl took the stage. She scanned the audience "a lookin' fer a feller." She poked fun at herself, mostly at her appearance.

"I once wore a mumu," she said. "I looked like a mama kangaroo with everybody home."

Then, the stage lights dimmed, and old ski nose himself stepped comfortably into the spotlight, cracking jokes and twirling a golf club.

"I wanted to be in show business since I was a boy," Hope told the audience. "I grew up with six brothers. That's how I learned to dance—waiting for the bathroom."

Right in the middle of Hope's act, Luckenbach's own Hondo Crouch came on stage and traded barbs with the Hollywood legend. They say Hope held his own.

At the end of the evening, Hope sang "Thanks for the Memory" and said a warm goodbye. He spent the night in Kerrville and played a round of golf at Riverhill Country Club before flying back to California.

The people in Fredericksburg still talk about the night Bob Hope came to town, but as a fundraiser, "Stars over the Hill Country" fell short of expectations.

The show broke even, but the publicity was priceless.

45

BOB HOPE MEETS
HONDO CROUCH

On a recent trip to Luckenbach, my wife and I sat under the oak trees, listened to the music and reminisced about the old days. As we walked past the bronze bust of legendary character Hondo Crouch, my wife recalled the time that Hondo stole the show from renowned entertainer Bob Hope.

Hope came to Fredericksburg on August 14, 1976, to raise money for the Admiral Nimitz Center. The actor, with the ski slope nose, met the admiral at Pearl Harbor in 1944 and kept in contact with Mrs. Nimitz, who had been living in California since the admiral's death.

At the time of his visit to the Texas Hill Country, Hope was one of the biggest stars in the world. Thanks to radio and television, everyone in America knew his name and recognized his image. He made over seventy films, and for six decades, he traveled the globe, entertaining American troops. A friend once said, "If he could live his life over, he wouldn't have time."

The day Bob Hope came to Fredericksburg began with a parade down *Hauptstrasse* (Main Street) from Kraus corner to the Nimitz Hotel. The grand marshal of the parade was Minnie Pearl. Miss Minnie, who was born Sarah Ophelia Colley, was a regular on the television show *Hee Haw* and a recent inductee into the Country Music Hall of Fame.

After the parade, the festivities moved to the Gillespie County Fairgrounds, where spectators enjoyed steer roping, barrel racing, food, beer and polka bands. That afternoon, Nashville recording artists Johnny Bush, Stoney Edwards and Darrell McCall performed on the stage in front of the

Hondo Crouch bust, Luckenbach. *Author's photograph.*

grandstand, followed by more food, beer and polka bands. Bruce Hathaway, the morning DJ at KTSA in San Antonio was the emcee. At 7:00 p.m., the Fredericksburg High School Band performed.

Bob Hope took the stage at eight o'clock that evening. He arrived in a golf cart as a fifteen-piece orchestra played in the background.

Hope twirled a golf club as he spoke into the microphone. His jokes and wisecracks came fast and furious. The upcoming presidential election, especially some of Jimmy Carter's recent comments about his religion, was his favorite target.

"I like to see politicians praying," Hope said. "It keeps their hands where you can see 'em."

Then, right in the middle of Hope's routine, Hondo Crouch walked on stage.

At the time, Hondo was one of two famous Americans born in the Texas Hill County (the other being Lyndon Johnson). Both men were in politics, in a manner of speaking. Johnson became president of the United States while Hondo was the self-proclaimed mayor of Luckenbach (population five).

Hondo had a colorful and unpredictable personality and a knack for self-promotion. His zany celebrations, like the Luckenbach World's Fair and the Return of the Mud Daubers, focused the nation's attention on his tiny town.

The World's Fair drew twenty thousand people. They consumed nine thousand cases of beer.

Someone once asked Hondo what he did for a living. "I write books on etiquette," he said while picking his nose. "But they don't sell too good."

On summer nights, he usually held court under the oak trees by the old general store in Luckenbach, but with an audience waiting for a world-famous entertainer just a few miles away, the temptation to make an appearance was too great.

Hondo came on stage unannounced in his usual dress: greasy jeans stuffed into a pair of well-worn boots, a sweat-stained cowboy hat, a red bandana, a scruffy white beard and an impish smile. He said he wanted to give Hope a new golf club but couldn't find one. "We don't play golf in Luckenbach." So, instead of a golf club, Hondo presented Hope with an axe handle.

"It doesn't have a head on it," Hondo explained. "It's hard to get 'ahead' in Luckenbach, so I'm just giving you the shaft."

Hope looked away in exasperation. Hondo smiled and waved. The crowd roared with laughter.

Six weeks later, Hondo Crouch died of a heart attack. Thanks for the memories.

46

MAKING HOUSE CALLS
WITH DR. KEIDEL

E arly doctors in Gillespie County didn't keep regular office hours. Many of the earliest doctors didn't even have offices. Doctoring, more often than not, was done at the homes of patients. House calls in the middle of the night were routine. A physician could be called into action at any time.

Dr. William Keidel, born in Hildesheim, Germany, came to Galveston, Texas, in 1845. From Galveston, he traveled to New Braunfels and then to Fredericksburg, where he was the Vereins doctor, the Adelsverein having promised the immigrants medical services in their contracts.

Dr. Keidel lived on Bear Creek, but on certain days, he would see patients in town. Whether there were one or two patients or a whole roomful, he received a $1.50 an afternoon for treating them.

Even Native Americans came to Dr. Keidel for treatment. Their way of paying him was to sneak up during the night and leave a dressed deer carcass or a wild turkey hanging from a tree in the yard.

At first, Dr. Keidel traveled everywhere on horseback, but around the start of the Civil War, he bought a buggy made by a wheelwright and upholsterer in Fredericksburg. The buggy had a black oilcloth top and was fairly waterproof.

People knew the days Dr. Keidel went to town. On those days, they would bring sick friends and family members out to meet him, and he would treat them there along the side of the road.

Dr. William Keidel's grandson Dr. Victor Keidel, born in Fredericksburg in 1882, borrowed money from Henry Klaerner to buy his first horse and saddle. Later, he bought a gig, a light two-wheeled wagon with a forked drawbar pulled by a single horse. The gig was high enough off the ground to clear most big rocks and stumps and ford most creeks without getting the driver's feet wet.

Dr. Victor Keidel liked to hunt, but doctoring took up most of his time. Sometimes, he tied his hounds to the axel of his gig and took them along so he could do a little hunting between house calls.

Dr. Victor Keidel was the first Gillespie County physician to own a car. He delivered over three thousand babies in his fifty-year career and couldn't afford to be slow in races with the stork.

His first car was an Overland, and it was the fifth car purchased in the county. The car's number, today's equivalent of a license plate, was "5."

The Keidel Memorial Hospital building, 258 East Main Street, Fredericksburg. *Author's photograph.*

Dr. Keidel kept the number 5 until state law regulated that license plate numbers changed.

A salesman sold Dr. Keidel on the idea of buying a car by telling him he could go out on a midnight call and be home in time for breakfast. But a car had its drawbacks. Dr. Keidel's car once sat in a mud hole for two weeks, bogged up to its axels, before the ground dried enough for a team of mules to drag it out.

One night, Dr. Victor Keidel made a house call to a sick man in Willow City. Woman's intuition told Mrs. Keidel (Clara Stieler) to go along.

On a particularly dangerous part of the road, the headlamps on the car went out, so Mrs. Keidel walked ahead of the car with a lantern. Then a storm came up, and the heavy rain put the lantern out.

Without a lantern, their visibility was down to zero. Sitting in their car through that dark and stormy night was like standing in a dark closet or at the bottom of a well.

To keep the car out of the ditch, Mrs. Keidel ran ahead as far as she could at each flash of lightning and called to Dr. Keidel, who drove to the sound of her voice. Then they would wait for the next lightning flash to go a little farther down the road.

Once, when the river was out, Dr. Victor Keidel drove his car across the Pedernales Railway Trestle to reach a critically ill patient on the other side. His passenger decided the crossing was too risky and stayed behind.

Doctoring in the early days of Gillespie County was always an adventure. Sometimes, getting there was an adventure itself.

47

FRANK VAN DER STUCKEN

Tenderly Poetic

Frank Van der Stucken is Fredericksburg's least known international celebrity. Many of us know his name but are unfamiliar with his work. As a composer and conductor of classical music, his compositions have a limited audience when compared to folk and popular music.

Van der Stucken's father, also named Frank, came to Texas from Antwerp, Belgium, with the French colonizer Henri Castro. In 1852, he married Sophie Schoenewolf of Fredericksburg.

The elder Van der Stucken ran a store on Main Street in Fredericksburg. When the Civil War broke out, he got a contract as a freighter. Later, he was a captain in the Confederate army and the chief justice of Gillespie County.

His son Frank Valentin Van der Stucken was born in Fredericksburg on October 15, 1858. The boy was baptized in the old Vereins Kirche.

Frank Van der Stucken's parents recognized his talent for music at an early age. The family moved back to Europe after the Civil War, in part so young Frank (who was probably eight or nine years old at the time) could pursue a musical career. There was little opportunity for classical training on the wild Texas frontier.

When the family left for Europe, Frank's father deeded his house, store and stable in Fredericksburg to his father-in-law. Back in Antwerp, the elder Van der Stucken went into the milling business and made a fortune.

Meanwhile, young Frank Van der Stucken studied music theory and composition with Belgian composer Pierre Benoit. He began performing his own compositions in public at the age of sixteen. He was one of the first

Frank Van der Stucken bust at Marketplatz, Fredericksburg. *Author's photograph.*

American musicians to be properly trained for the career of a Kapellmeister (professional orchestral conductor).

Van der Stucken admired the German composer Richard Wagner, and his compositions sometimes used texts from Goethe and other German writers.

Between 1878 and 1881, Van der Stucken traveled across Austria, Switzerland, Italy and France. He hung out with Italian composer Giuseppe Verdi in Paris. He married German singer Maria Vollmer in 1880. He met her in Paris, where she was a student.

In 1881, the Hungarian pianist, composer and conductor Franz Liszt invited Van der Stucken to Weimar and insisted the young man give concerts of his own works.

In 1884, Van der Stucken came back to America to direct the Arion Society, a famous New York men's choir. While in New York, he conducted the American premier of Brahms's third symphony. He helped organize the Northeast German Saenger Bund, putting together spectacular concerts featuring massive choirs of four thousand to five thousand voices.

He fought all his life for the recognition of American musicians at home and abroad. In New York City, he conducted the first concert in America devoted exclusively to American composers. In 1889, he conducted the first concert of American compositions in Europe at the Paris World Exposition.

In 1895, First Lady Helen Taft founded the Cincinnati Symphony Orchestra and convinced Frank Van der Stucken to organize and direct it. He held the job for the next eight years.

In his spare time, Van der Stucken led the Boston Symphony Orchestra, the Chicago Symphony Orchestra and the New York Philharmonic as a guest conductor. He directed the Cincinnati May Music Fest from 1906 to 1912. The May Fest featured the full Cincinnati Symphony Orchestra and a grand chorus of several hundred voices. It grew out of the German *Saengerfest*.

By the turn of the twentieth century, Frank Van der Stucken had carved out a name for himself as an internationally known composer and director. The *Indianapolis Journal*, on April 25, 1897, called him "one of the few really great directors and conductors of the world," adding that he was "an all-around conductor of extraordinary merit."

The *Washington Evening Star* (May 20, 1923) described his music as ranging from "riots of color and emotion" to "tenderly poetic."

I listened to Frank Van der Stucken's music on YouTube and found it a complex, mysterious and wonderful language. I don't speak it very well, but I enjoy the way it makes me feel and admire the magic it takes to create it.

48

FELIX PEHL AND HIS
OLD-TIME BAND

T he music was sometimes called oompah—the *oom* coming from the thumping cadence of the tuba rattling the air and the *pah* from the lilting tones of the trombones, trumpets and accordions jumping in on the offbeat. Not only could you hear the music a half-mile away, but you could also feel the deep notes of the tuba vibrate in your chest.

And the music was surprisingly easy to dance to, even for a klutz like me, with two left feet and the rhythm of a corpse. Not that the dancing was particularly graceful or even dignified, but it was more fun than a barrel of Shiner Bock.

The culture of a place is expressed in its customs, language, food and art. Felix Pehl and his Old Time Band expressed the culture of the German Hill Country in music.

The waltzes they played were peasant dances from Austria and southern Germany. European nobility preferred the more stately minuet and considered the waltz to be low-class and vulgar.

But the waltz caught on. The sweeping popularity of the waltz and its variants was a cultural affirmation of the declining influence of the nobility and the rising power of the European middle class.

The schottische was a variation of the waltz, but the most popular offshoot was the polka. By the 1840s, the polka was the most popular dance in Europe.

Felix Theodore Pehl loved music, and he was proud of his German heritage. He learned the polka and other German folk music from the working-class Germans who brought them from Germany to the Texas Hill Country.

Pehl began playing in bands in 1916. He formed his first band in 1925 out of necessity. He owned the dance hall in Albert and needed a band to play there.

Dance halls were part of Hill Country culture for much of the twentieth century. Every Saturday night at dance halls all over this part of Texas, adults danced and socialized while the children played and then went to sleep on quilts in the corner.

Soon, Felix Pehl and his band were playing gigs somewhere every weekend. At first, they rode to dances on horseback with their instruments tied to their saddles.

Pehl's Old Time Band played at Peter's Hall in Fredericksburg, Weinheimer's Hall in Stonewall, Tatsch's Hall in Cain City, Engel's Hall in Luckenbach, Deike's Hall in Hye, the Handy Stop in Bankersmith, Ottmer's Hall, Baron's Creek Hall and Seipp's Pavilion. They sometimes played a Saturday night dance as far away as San Antonio, but it's possible they wouldn't get home until late Sunday afternoon if it rained and the creek was out.

Later, Pehl's Old Time Band played at Wurstfest in New Braunfels and Octoberfest in Anhalt. They were headliners at Night in Old Fredericksburg.

The rowdies didn't get too far out of line at their dances—not with Gillespie County sheriff Hugo Klaerner and Fredericksburg mayor Sidney Henke in the band.

Look closely at the photograph on page 153, and you will notice that the accordion is upside down. After an accident left Arthur Klein with only one finger on his right hand, he flipped the instrument upside down so he could play the keyboard with his left hand.

Felix Pehl and the band played at the Institute of Texan Cultures in San Antonio, the State Fair of Texas in Dallas and on special occasions for President Lyndon Johnson in Stonewall. In 1975, the band traveled to Washington, D.C., at the invitation of the Smithsonian, to play at the Festival of American Folk Life.

The band's instruments were just as iconic as the music they played. Sheriff Klaerner's E-Flat tuba saw duty in his father Alfred Klaerner's famed Bunkusville Band. Some of the instruments, dented and tarnished, dated to the early days of Fredericksburg.

Few of the band members, if any, could read music, but they memorized a sixty-five-song repertoire, including polkas, schottisches, waltzes and even

Felix Pehl's Old Time Band. *Gillespie County Historical Society.*

a few showtunes. They may have hit a sour note every now and then, but no one seemed to mind.

Musical perfection wasn't the goal. This was about having fun—for the band as well as the audience. It was *Gemütlichkeit* put to music.

For a half-century Felix Pehl, the maestro, and his Old Time Band delighted audiences. Then, one by one, their lungs and hearts gave, out and the music faded, leaving only memories of good times, lilting notes and vibrations in the air.

49

Adolph Stieler

The Goat King

S tieler Hill is the high point on the road between Fredericksburg and
Comfort. At the top of the hill is the headquarters of the Stieler
Ranch, which was once home to Adolph Stieler, the Goat King.
Adolph Stieler was born into the ranching business, with the blood of
three famous ranch families flowing in his veins. His grandfather on his
mother's side was Caspar Real, who came to Kerr County in the 1850s.
Real married Emelie Schreiner, one of Captain Charles Schreiner's sisters.

Caspar Real imported Delaine sheep from Ohio. He shipped them down
the Mississippi River by riverboat to New Orleans, by steam ship to Indianola
and then by wagon to his ranch in Kerr County.

Hermann Stieler, Adolph's father, was born in Germany but came to Kerr
County to work as a freighter for Captain Schreiner. On January 1, 1877,
Hermann married Emma Real, Caspar and Emelie's daughter.

In the 1870s, Hermann took up three sections of land in the Hill Country
near Comfort. He retired in 1917 and turned his sheep ranch, then covering
twenty-five sections, over to his sons

In 1921, Adolph Stieler borrowed money against a life insurance policy to
buy eight hundred angora goats. His neighbors thought he was crazy. At the
time, goats sold for twenty-five to fifty cents apiece. Mohair sold for six cents
a pound. The goat business was the fast lane to the poorhouse.

But Adolph saw the big picture and had an uncanny feel for the flow
of the nation's economy. He saw that automobile manufacturers were

Adolph Stieler's gate sign, Stieler Hill, Comfort Highway. *Author's photograph.*

beginning to make upholstery out of mohair. Clothing manufacturers were using more mohair to make suits, coats, dresses and sweaters. Mohair prices were beginning to rise.

Adolph Stieler held the course, and by 1942, he owned thirty-eight thousand goats, twenty thousand sheep and one thousand cattle grazing on ninety thousand acres in Kendall, Kimble, Kerr, Gillespie, Blanco and San Saba Counties.

Adolph was a skilled stockman who knew how to manage the range. He studied the grazing patterns of goats, sheep, cattle and deer, and he used his knowledge to get the most out of each pasture without overgrazing it.

In 1942, as war raged in Europe and the Pacific, *Life Magazine* sent renowned photographer Alfred Eisenstaedt to Stieler Hill to visit the Goat King. This was three years before Eisenstaedt took his most famous picture, that of the kissing sailor and the nurse in Times Square on VJ Day.

Life Magazine introduced the Goat King and his subjects to the world. "Goats are among man's oldest friends," *Life* told its readers.

> *Goats are mentioned 137 times in the Bible....Angoras are the blue-blooded elite of the goat world. Their long, curly, silky fleece, known commercially as mohair, is used to make fine upholstery, yarn and fabrics....Angora goats are dainty, shy and not at all smelly. Their fleece is so rich in healthy oil (lanolin), that goat men who handle them a lot have pink, soft hands like a baby's.*

When the American economy took off after the war, the price of mohair soared. By 1950, mohair sold for eighty-five cents a pound. Angoras sold for fifteen to sixteen dollars apiece. Adolph Stieler was a wealthy man.

Adolph Stieler's grave, Comfort German Cemetery, Comfort. *Author's photograph.*

Stieler's first wife died in 1936. In 1955, he married Merle Porter of Austin. Their reception was held in the Crystal Ballroom at the Driskill Hotel. They honeymooned in New Orleans, Miami and Havana.

Adolph Stieler was a dyed-in-the-wool Republican. On January 20, 1952, he traveled to Washington, D.C., to attend the inauguration of his friend Dwight Eisenhower, and he was a delegate to the 1956 Republican Convention.

In 1956, Mrs. Stieler made a gift for Mamie Eisenhower: a lime green felt skirt adorned with felt elephants and the words "There's nothing wrong in Texas that Ike and a little rain won't cure."

On August 9, 1969, local Republicans honored Mr. and Mrs. Stieler with a reception at Louise Hayes Park in Kerrville. The main speaker was another Stieler friend, Congressman George H.W. Bush from Houston. At the end of his speech, Bush stood with Adolph Stieler on the podium—the future president of the United States and the Goat King of Stieler Hill.

50

FRED GIPSON'S TREASURES

Since it was my day to read to fourth graders, I walked into Mrs. Stehling's classroom looking for a copy of *Old Yeller*. She handed me a well-worn and appropriately dog-eared hardback from the shelf behind her desk.

This was no ordinary copy of the American classic. It was signed by the author. Twenty-five years later, I still remember holding that treasure in my hand and thinking that was as close as I would ever get to Fred Gipson, the author and one of my heroes.

Gipson's parents, Beck and Emma Gipson, came to Mason County from deep East Texas in a horse-drawn wagon. Before leaving the Piney Woods, Beck Gipson carefully packed an alligator egg in a wooden chest. The egg hatched not long after the family reached the Llano River. It must have been the first and maybe the only alligator hatched in Mason County.

Fred Gipson was born in Mason County in 1908. He didn't care for school, but like his father, he had an uncommon curiosity about the natural world. He liked to fish and hunt with his dogs. He heard old-timers tell stories about Mason County and developed a remarkable understanding of the Hill Country and its people.

Gipson graduated from Mason High School in 1926. He studied journalism at the University of Texas but left after three years to make some money as a newspaperman.

Then, in the 1940s, Fred Gipson took a giant leap of faith. He quit his regular job, and the small yet regular paycheck that went with it, to write magazine articles and fiction.

Left: Old Yeller statue, public library, Mason. *Author's photograph.*

Below: *Old Yeller* book. *Author's photograph.*

He made $150 in his first year as a freelancer. "If I knew then what I know now," he told a friend, "I would not have had the nerve to have tried writing."

But daring and persistence paid off. Beginning in 1946, Fred Gipson published a string of successful books, including *Fabulous Empire*, *Hound Dog Man*, *The Home Place*, *Cowhand*, *The Trail Driving Rooster*, *Recollection Creek*, *Big Bend*, *Old Yeller* and *Savage Sam*.

Gipson wrote a gentler style of fiction than most modern-day Texas novelists. Walter Prescott Webb compared Gipson to Mark Twain. Both Gipson and Twain wrote stories with universal appeal. J. Frank Dobie doubted Gipson's talent but came around.

Gipson wrote *Old Yeller*, his masterpiece, in three months. The coming-of-age story about a young man, an old yellow dog and little Arliss swimming naked in the drinkin' water was an instant best-seller.

For years, *Old Yeller* sold more copies than any other book written by a Texan. It is a rare and authentic story that continues to entertain and touch hearts over half a century after Gipson wrote it.

Four of Gipson's books became movies. The movie *Old Yeller*, produced by Walt Disney and starring Dorothy McGuire, Fess Parker and Tommy Kirk, premiered in San Angelo in 1957. The story takes the audience on an emotional rollercoaster ride.

"We blubbered through the whole dang thing," said Kerrville cartoonist Ace Reid after seeing the movie. "Six people drowned in the first three rows."

But literary and financial success did not bring happiness to Fred Gipson. His life wasn't easy. With each new book, he worried he might never be published again.

After the tragic death of his son, Gipson turned to Scotch to comfort his broken heart. He was always ornery and opinionated, but when he drank whiskey, he was really hard to get along with. His wife left him. His friends and neighbors couldn't stand to be around him. Alcoholism, paranoia, depression and a lack of confidence haunted him the rest of his life.

It is sad and ironic to think that this man who brought so much joy and meaning to my life spent his last years bitter and alone.

He died on August 14, 1973, at his Recollection Creek Ranch. He was buried on a hillside in the State Cemetery in Austin next to his friend Walter Prescott Webb.

I still remember the thrill of holding that autographed copy of *Old Yeller*. But the real treasures Fred Gipson left us can be found in his timeless stories of West Texas. They are hilarious, heartbreaking and ultimately hopeful.

51

ALFRED GILES

Texas Architect

A lfred Giles was an English architect and an unlikely Texan, but he had a profound influence on building design in San Antonio and helped define the architectural style most associated with the Texas Hill Country.

Giles was born in London in 1850. He studied architecture at King's College but left England for a healthier climate after a bout with rheumatic fever. The damp London air was bad for his health.

So, in 1873, Giles came to Texas. He set up shop in downtown San Antonio, at 114 West Houston Street.

Over the next four decades, he designed between ninety and one hundred of the most beautiful buildings in South Texas and northern Mexico. He designed county courthouses for Bexar, Brooks, El Paso, Gillespie, Guadalupe, Kendall, Kerr, Kimble, Live Oak, Webb and Wilson Counties. He drew the plans for several homes in the historic King William District in San Antonio and the 1909 addition to the Menger Hotel next door to the Alamo.

Giles left his mark all over the Texas Hill Country, a place he came to love. In Fredericksburg, he designed the Gillespie County Courthouse (now the Pioneer Memorial Library), the William Bierschwale House at 110 North Bowie Street and the Bank of Fredericksburg on Main Street (now Kowert Real Estate). He also designed the Morris Ranch School House.

In Kerrville, Giles designed the Charles Schreiner Mansion, the A.C. Schreiner Jr. residence, the Schreiner Store and the Schreiner Bank. In

The 1881 Gillespie County Courthouse, designed by Alfred Giles. *Author's photograph.*

Comfort, he designed the August Faltin Building, the Old Comfort Post Office, the Ingenhuett-Faust Hotel, the Ingenhuett-Karger Saloon and the Paul Ingenhuett residence.

His buildings are timeless, and yet they reflect the time and place in which they were built. His style was Victorian with Spanish and German influences.

His Hill Country residences, with their native limestone walls, large windows, narrow breezy rooms, deep porches and rustic ironworks, are pitch perfect reflections of nineteenth-century Texas Hill Country culture. His public buildings express strength, trust and permanence.

Giles had a deep respect for the Alamo defenders and designed a 163-foot-tall monument to honor them. Mrs. Maury Maverick and most of the city leaders in San Antonio supported the construction of the Giles monument, but the selection committee chose instead the *Cenotaph* (empty tomb), designed by Pompeo Coppini.

The backers of the Giles's design were not kind to the *Cenotaph*. J. Frank Dobie said the Coppini monument, the one that now stands in Alamo Plaza, looked like "a grain silo."

Hillingdon gate, Old
San Antonio Road.
Author's photograph.

Alfred Giles returned to London in 1885, but in less than a year, he was back in Texas. His time away from the Lone Star State made him realize that he had become a Texan through and through. He missed the Hill Country and couldn't wait to get back to it.

Giles bought a thirteen-thousand-acre cattle and sheep ranch near Comfort. He called it Hillingdon after his birthplace in England. He lived at the ranch and was active in its daily operations. He was a member of the Texas Cattle Raiser's Association and a founding member of the Texas Sheep and Goat Raiser's Association.

When Giles traveled from Hillingdon to San Antonio, he rode either a horse or carriage to Comfort. He then took the Guadalupe Stage Line to Boerne and the San Antonio and Aransas Pass Railroad to San Antonio.

He carried two homing pigeons with him. He released one to let his wife know he had arrived safely in San Antonio and the other to announce his plans for return.

Alfred Giles died at Hillingdon Ranch on August 13, 1920. He was buried beside his wife in San Antonio City Cemetery.

He made our world more beautiful.

52

THE MUD DAUBERS RETURN
TO LUCKENBACH

O n March 19, 1977, at 2:30 in the afternoon, a lone mud dauber flew in low over South Grape Creek, darted around for a few minutes and came in for a landing on an empty beer can. The crowd of eight thousand went wild, scaring the daylights out of the nervous little critter that immediately lit out in the direction of Cain City.

You know those people in Luckenbach. Any flimsy excuse to throw a beer party.

The idea for the "Mud Dauber Fest," or, more formally, "When the Mud Daubers Come Back to Luckenbach Day," may have come from a letter that Hondo Crouch wrote to Elizabeth Taylor in 1976, inviting the famous actress to come to Luckenbach. For some unexplainable reason, Hondo began extolling the artistic genius of mud daubers:

> *If you like mud daubers Liz, you'll be ecstatic. Luckenbach is the mud dauber capital of the world. We've just got mud dauber sculptures everywhere. Some of it is just breathtaking, and some of it is a little obscene, so we try to keep it out of sight of the children.*
>
> *They will really go all out if you come. We're resting them up right now (their daubers get sore), but they'll be out there just daubing away in September.*
>
> *I sure hope you can come. A Luckenbach moon can make even an ugly girl look pretty. Think of what it can do for a beauty like you.*

Luckenbach Store. *Author's photograph.*

When Hondo died later that year, the resident characters in Luckenbach took the mud dauber idea and ran with it.

"Every March 19, the mud daubers come back to Luckenbach," spokesman Jack Harmon explained. "They come back—swarms of 'em—all rested up, ready to put their little daubers to work creating wonderful mud sculptures."

It was no accident that the Mud Dauber Fest fell on March 19, the same day the swallows returned to San Juan Capistrano in California. The motive was revenge. It seems Texans were still bent out of shape about the organizers of the World Chili Cookoff moving the event from Terlingua to Hollywood.

"Everything would have been alright if they hadn't messed with our chili." Jack Harmon said.

Luckenbach mayor Kathy Morgan invited President Carter's brother Billy to the Mud Dauber Fest to serve as mayor for a day. A lot of people felt sorry for Billy, who had just lost his second bid for mayor of Plains, Georgia.

Opting not to pay the first brother's traveling expenses, "since it might look like influence peddling," the mayor instead offered Billy all the beer he could drink. If you remember Billy, it might have been cheaper to pay his traveling expenses.

But the mayor withdrew the invitation after calling Billy's home, his service station and his peanut warehouse in Plains and getting no answer. "That's OK," she declared. "We'll just have that much more beer to drink."

The mayor's office was flooded with offers to take Billy's place, given the same terms.

The Mud Dauber Fest began when the mayor poured a bottle of melted snow from Buffalo, New York, into the creek as a gesture of friendship between Luckenbach and its sister city on Lake Erie. The relationship between Luckenbach and Buffalo came from all the publicity Buffalo received in a contest at the Mud Dauber Fest. It was a song writing competition about the mud daubers returning to Luckenbach. The winner got nothing. The loser got a free trip to Buffalo in January.

Another event was washer pitching on the beautifully manicured playing surface located in the sticker patch on the high ground along South Grape Creek.

Vendors peddled, among other things, leftover bicentennial souvenirs, giving manufacturers "one last chance to rip off the public." Ten percent of all sales went to the Hondo Crouch "I told You So" Memorial Fund.

The Mud Dauber Fest drew a large crowd. Beer flowed like rainwater through a storm drain, and there was a funny-smelling smoke in the air. The multitude waited all day for the mud daubers.

Only one dauber showed up, and he didn't stay long.

53

The Luckenbach World's Fair

The vicious nature of current political discourse makes me nauseous. We have lost—temporarily, I hope—the ability to laugh at ourselves and each other. What this self-righteous world needs is some inspired silliness.

I miss the Luckenbach World's Fair.

The World's Fair began as a harebrained idea from the minds of Luckenbach's owners, Hondo Crouch and Guich Koock, but as usual with those guys, the initial idea was only a point of departure. It was followed by a hard left turn into a bizarre world of humorous nonsense.

"We're planning on twenty thousand to thirty thousand people this first year," Koock stated, tongue in cheek, when he announced the first World's Fair in the summer of 1973.

The town, of course, wasn't equipped to handle a crowd much larger than a beach volleyball team. Five pickup trucks in town at one time would cause a bottleneck. Luckenbach was not designed for modern vehicular traffic.

At least there was hope that the Luckenbach parking meter, an important source of city revenue, would get a workout. Not that anyone ever paid to park in Luckenbach, but every once in a while, a drunk cowboy dropped a quarter in, thinking it was a slot machine.

Guich and Hondo dreamed up the World's Fair as an elaborate joke, hoping to bring some business to their little town, but the joke backfired. Ten thousand people showed up.

The store ran out of beer. There weren't enough toilets—or trees.

People, as it turned out, were longing for a little foolishness in a world that was way too serious for its own good.

The political atmosphere in 1973 was strangely similar to our current mess. Richard Nixon and the Watergate scandal dominated the news. The country was politically polarized.

America needed a diversion. So, the news of the World's Fair spread like gossip at a beauty parlor. Newspapers all over the Southwest picked up the story.

The first World's Fair had an art show featuring Fredericksburg artist Charles Beckendorf and Jim Franklin of Austin. Franklin painted surreal posters of armadillos and prairie schooners inside Lone Star Beer bottles.

But the Luckenbach World's Fair was more than an art show. It was part *Animal House* and part *Willie's Picnic*. In addition to art and beer, there was a tobacco spitting contest, judged on distance and accuracy, and a buffalo chip tossing contest.

The crowd, as a whole, was well behaved. "At least," Guich Koock reported, "there wasn't much beer drinking during Sunday morning gospel singing."

There was talk of a second World's Fair in 1974, but the Luckenbach Chamber of Commerce decided against it. The hangover from the first one lasted longer than expected.

The first year's crowd was so large, it scared the livestock. The cows stopped giving milk, and the chickens quit laying eggs. The guineas disappeared entirely.

So, after a yearlong hiatus, Crouch and Koock staged the second semiannual Luckenbach World's Fair at the old fairgrounds in Fredericksburg. In addition to music, drinking, spitting and tossing, there was a championship chicken flying contest, a laughing contest and thoroughbred armadillo races.

Hondo Crouch was the perfect host. As one visitor put it, "Just looking at Hondo put you in a good mood."

No one knew what to expect from Hondo. One day, he showed up in a suit; he said he ran out of dirty clothes.

After one more year in Fredericksburg, the World's Fair moved back to Luckenbach. In addition to the usual events, there was a new contest called the "Back Door Races." At the sound of a shotgun, four contestants, dressed in their underwear, had to jump out of bed and put on their pants. The first one through the window was the winner.

There were disappointments. The Russian Olympic team never made it. They were entered in the vodka chugging contest. Technically, they weren't no-shows, since they never responded to the official invitation.

Luckenbach World's Fair poster. *Jimmy Reichenau.*

The last Luckenbach World's Fair was held in 1981. By then, Hondo had died, and Guich had gone to purgatory (also known as Hollywood).

Years have passed, and the world has turned serious again. We've lost our appreciation for the absurd.

I hope we get it back.

A Night for the Ages at Cherry Spring Tavern

It was business as usual the night Elvis Presley wiggled across the stage at Cherry Spring Tavern. After all, there was a time when just about any hillbilly troubadour who ever wore a Nudie suit made the bone-jarring, butt-numbing bus ride to this legendary dance hall, eighteen miles northwest of Fredericksburg.

The king of rock and roll wasn't even a prince in October 1955. The local newspaper misspelled his name. Only in hindsight did the magnitude of the evening sink in.

Although Cherry Spring (sometimes spelled Cherry Springs) hasn't hosted a dance in years, the energy of a thousand Saturday nights still surges through the place. For me, the memories are as thick as weeds in the parking lot. I can still see the long wooden tables and the wagon wheel chandeliers. I can smell the sawdust, the cigarette smoke and the perfume as strong as tear gas.

By the time I first swaggered through the door at Cherry Spring Tavern, locals had been gathering there for almost one hundred years. Herman Lehmann operated the first tavern at Cherry Spring beginning in 1889. Lehmann, the adopted son of Comanche chief Quanah Parker, was a bona fide Texas legend. He was the second most famous Native American captive in Texas after Quanah's mother, Cynthia Ann.

In 1926, Alfred Klingelhoefer built a wooden dance hall at the current site. In 1946, a new owner added gas heat, indoor plumbing and flush toilets.

What never changed was the reason people went there. They went to dance.

Texas music is dancing music, road tested for its durability in dance halls, taverns, honky-tonks, roadhouses and juke joints from Texarkana to El Paso. It rose up from the cotton fields, the swamps and the dusty plains of West Texas.

The very personality of Texas Music is to serve the dancers. That's why Bob Wills added drums and Ernest Tubb used electric instruments—the better to dance to in noisy beer joints.

Dance music was always front and center at Cherry Spring Tavern. Czech-German swing artist Adolph Hofner and his Pearl Wranglers were practically the house band from the 1940s to the 1980s.

Mostly regional acts played Cherry Spring until Ruth and Martin Kuykendall bought the place in the early 1950s. Enlarged and remodeled in the summer of 1952, Cherry Spring Tavern was all spiffed up and ready to swing into the spotlight with the biggest names in country music.

Bob Wills was already a star when he and his Texas Playboys took the stage at Cherry Spring Tavern for the first time on April 30, 1952. Flamboyant honky-tonk singer Webb Pierce was the headliner on November 26, 1952. Red Sovine was the opening act. I don't believe Hank Williams played there,

Cherry Spring Dancehall, Cherry Spring. *Author's photograph.*

but his widow did on February 10, 1953. It was barely a month after old Hank died, full of booze and pills in the backseat of his Cadillac, somewhere on a lost highway in West Virginia.

The Maddox Brothers and Rose, a legendary California band, played Cherry Spring Tavern on March 3, 1953. The Maddox Brothers and Rose, influenced by blues, jazz and swing, played a unique and unforgettable style of country boogie, an early form of rockabilly. They laid the foundation for the Bakersfield Sound. Buck Owens and Merle Haggard idolized them. A case can be made that Fred Maddox, while slapping his upright bass, played some of the first notes of rock and roll.

Cherry Spring Tavern hosted Lefty Frizzell on March 14, 1953. Marty Robbins played there on September 16, 1953. Gentleman Jim Reeves took the stage on July 29, 1953. The not yet famous Andrews Sisters closed out 1953 with a New Year's Eve show. On February 17, 1954, couples danced to Hank Thompson and the Brazos Valley Boys for $1.50 each.

But October 9, 1955, was a night for the ages. That Sunday, Martin and Ruth Kuykendall booked a traveling show that was sponsored by the Louisiana Hayride and radio station KWKH in Shreveport.

The first man off the bus was Horace "Hoss" Logan, the founder of the Louisiana Hayride. Next came recording artists Jimmy and Johnny, Dalton and Little Jo, Betty Amos and future star Johnny Horton. Those were the opening acts.

The headliner was a three-man band featuring future Rock and Roll Hall of Fame guitarist Scotty Moore, bassist Bill Black, and a twenty-year-old swivel-hipped truck driver from Tupelo, Mississippi.

The now-famous advertisement in the *Fredericksburg Standard* called him Clovis Presley. At the time, no one noticed, but in a year, Elvis would be the most famous entertainer in the world.

BIG SHOW AND
DANCE
K. W. K. H's.
LOUISIANA HAYRIDE
Entire Cast in Person,
Clovis Presley
With Scotty and Bill, Jimmy and Johnny, Johnny Horton, Betty Amos, Dalton and Little Jo, Billy Birdbrain (comedian) Horace Logan, M. C.
Producer of
LOUISIANA HAYRIDE
Eleven Great Artists, along with ELVIS PRESLEY'S BAND
Cherry Springs Tavern
SUNDAY NIGHT, OCT. 9th
Starting 8:00 P. M.
Admission: $1.50.

Opposite: Clovis Presley advertisement. *From the* Fredericksburg Standard.

Above: Cherry Spring stage. *Author's photograph.*

The young musicians made quite an impression on Ruth Kuykendall. She described Elvis as "the nicest person, except Johnny Horton, who I bossed around as if he had been my son."

While the night with Elvis was hard to top, Cherry Spring Tavern came close. George Jones played there at least twice—on time and relatively sober.

Other *Grand Ole Opry* stars who made the trip out the Mason Highway included Ernest Tubb, Ray Price, Faron Young, Floyd Cramer, Hank Locklin, Slim Whitman, Claude King, Doug Kershaw, Little Jimmie Dickens, Johnny Bush, Gene Watson and the Midnight Cowboy Bill Mack.

On March 12, 1955, Cherry Spring welcomed saxophonist King Perry and his orchestra. Big Daddy Pat and his famous eight-piece orchestra played a show there on May 16, 1959. Perhaps a dozen Black acts performed at Cherry Spring Tavern in the 1940s and 1950s.

Skin color didn't seem to be a factor at Cherry Spring. What mattered was the music. It was a rare attitude you wouldn't expect to find in rural Texas in the racially charged 1950s.

When Martin Kuykendall got sick in 1962, he and Ruth sold the tavern. They booked Bob Wills to play the last show, but Bob had a heart attack and had to cancel. The heyday of Cherry Spring Tavern was over.

A series of caretakers ran Cherry Spring over the next twenty-five years, but crowds were harder to draw in. There was too much competition from other forms of entertainment. Operating costs increased. The rural location that once drew dancing fools from four counties became a liability.

Cherry Spring Tavern, where the Hillbilly Cat once shook the rafters, is quiet now. The only sounds are the furious rush of cars and trucks barreling down Highway 87 and the wind whistling ghostly tunes through broken window panes.

There are rumors that this iconic old dance hall will be restored. I hope the rumors are true. A lot of history was written on the stage where Elvis once played before he was king, back when rock and roll was still in the shadows, somewhere between country and western and rhythm and blues.

ABOUT THE AUTHOR

Michael Barr earned a bachelor's degree in history and government from the University of Texas at Austin and a master's degree in history and government from Texas State University. He was a teacher and a principal in Fredericksburg, Johnson City and Gatesville. His books include *Remembering Bulldog Turner: Unsung Monster of the Midway, Cloyce Box: 6'4" and Bulletproof* and *Rope Burns and Lead Poisoning: Stories of Western Mentality, Throat Disease and the Open Range.* His articles have appeared in *Old West Magazine, True West Magazine, Southwestern Historical Quarterly, Texas Highways Magazine* and *Rock and Vine Magazine.* His Hindsights column appears in the *Fredericksburg Standard,* the *Johnson City Record-Courier* and TexasEscapes.com.

Visit us at
www.historypress.com